W9-BRB-153

Cover design by Ijlal Munir
Author photograph by Rodney Wright
Edited by Jason Mortensen

I have tried to recreate events, locales and conversations from my memories of them. In order to maintain their anonymity in some instances I have changed the names of individuals.

theproperperception.com

ISBN 978-0-9915746-0-5

Acknowledgements

First of all I'd like to thank the Creator of the heavens and the earth to whom all praise is due for His mercy and His guidance and for keeping me sane and faithful throughout my entire prison experience. I also thank Him for the peaceful and productive environment He placed me in when I returned home that enabled me to stay focused while I pursued a college degree and wrote this book.

I thank my parents for the protective environment in which they provided for me and my siblings, my father for supporting the activities that I was involved in as a child, and my mother. How do you thank a mother for love, creativity, empathy, sympathy, education, encouragement, courage, establishing faith, and bringing to life the ideas in your head so that they become a material reality? That's what my mother did for me and I will forever be greatful.

I'd like to thank my brothers and sisters: Amia, Bashir, Nisaa, Ibn, and Saddiqa for their unwavering support throughout my life especially in my greatest time of need as well as providing any help I needed, without question, as I made the transition back into society. Thank you. I love you all.

I'd like to thank my entire family, grandmother, aunts, uncles, cousins, nephew (Leo, its only you so far buddy) nieces'(Laila and Neeya) family/friends (Almetheia, your feedback was valuable) and in-laws who embraced me and supported me in writing this book and never second-guessed me and had absolute faith in my ability. My support team was truly an all-star cast.

Saving the best for last I'd like to thank my wonderful, wonderful wife Carrie who introduced herself to me through a letter and remained by my side for the remaining six years of my sentence. She faithfully and courageously invited a man who had just spent 15 years in prison into her and her child's life, A man who had no social skills, no relationship skills, no work skills or work history, a partial education, and a bunch of ideas about everything. I do not believe that there is another woman who would have embraced me to the degree in which she did with me in such a condition. I love you Carrie and our two beautiful daughters, Imani and Amina.

This book is dedicated to the mothers, fathers, teachers, principals, clergy, and community workers who are determined to keep our sons and daughters from ever stepping foot inside of the penitentiary.

Table Of Contents

Preface

Every day during my fifteen long, long years in prison, I watched hope get snatched away from men who had very little to no faith. In fact, the men with no faith were the ones who were most angry and easily aggravated. They had not yet figured out how to deflect, how to shield, or how to protect their minds from the mistreatment, hatred, and intentional aggravation from people who could not have cared less if they lived or died.

Many books have been written about men's experiences in prison, however the complete understanding is what is necessary if young lives are to be saved. This devastating reality must be clearly explained and given the proper perception, without any romanticism or glorification. It is a war within. I had to wage a mental and spiritual war within myself to keep from becoming influenced by an environment that can completely desensitize people so much that they become creatures and not men.

An inmate I knew and played baseball with every summer in the prison league took all he was going to take from a guard who treated prisoners like insects. One day after insulting another inmate, as was his norm, the officer got up from his desk and went to the bathroom, leaving behind the beverage he was drinking. Vulgarly, in front of everyone who was in the dayroom, this man walked up to the desk, grabbed the officers drink, and filled it with his urine.

It is not only the frustration from staff and administrations of penitentiaries that helps shape prisoners' attitudes but also the policies and designs of institutions that strain the senses and heavily contribute to sensory deprivation.

Every time a visitor came to see me, I would look at the different colors in his or her clothes. The microwaved food from the vending machines smelled and tasted the way my mother cooked, not the flavorless, soy-based meals I ate three times a day. In prison there are no vivid colors, caressing touches, warm embraces, or gentle words; there is no consideration of another's feelings and no empathy, and nothing is soft. It's either concrete or metal, and it's all gray, gloomy, and dismal. Now add the insane lunatics, thieves, rapists, killers, white supremacists, child molesters, pimps, meth-heads, crackheads, dope fiends, prostitutes, scheming and conniving con men, and a wild, lawless, heartless, fatherless, desensitized, lost generation of young men. This is the world I entered at twenty years old, having been raised by both parents, with a brother and two sisters who graduated from college, and my youngest brother a sergeant in the United States Air Force.

I was raised with five siblings in a modest two-parent household on the south side of Chicago. For ten years we lived in an apartment community complex called Concordia Park, in walking distance from Eden Green, Golden Gates, and Altgeld Gardens. I had a good time growing up in that area. There were many other children the same ages as my brothers, sisters, and me, and like most children we got into it all. We were just as mischievous as other kids, and we egged the buses and lit packs of firecrackers on people's porches at night and ran. But we were good kids. Some of my best memories come from that old neighborhood; however, concerns about a declining community made my parents buy a home and move us to Dolton, Illinois, a neighboring suburb of Chicago.

In 1987 Dolton was a nice, quiet, family-friendly environment with a good high school and good grammar and middle schools. My siblings and I received love and support for any activities we were involved in as children. Our mother, a determined, hard-working, God-fearing woman, saw to it that her children were not only well provided for but also instilled with the core principles of human decency that helped develop us into the adults we have become. My mother did her job well because we were safe, but that safety still did not stop me from making the terrible choices that would devastate my family and send me to the penitentiary.

I have never lived in at-risk neighborhoods, and I was raised in a loving, supportive family. My parents did not drink alcohol or use drugs of any kind. So how did this happen to me? What influences did I allow into my life that replaced the positive influences of my family and surroundings? This is the story of a young man, whose parents did everything right, ended up in the penitentiary and had to endure the vicious and demoralizing culture of prison and its harmful influences.

I went to high school all four years and had a ball. My freshman year I was a three-sport athlete with a promising future in athletics, but my laziness in the classroom kept me ineligible after that. My brother and several of our friends were big-time college recruits who hung out together and kept each other out of serious trouble. Even though I was surrounded by great players, it wasn't enough to motivate me to improve my grades. It wasn't until the end of the second semester of my senior year that I truly found myself lost. I had been doing just enough to get by my entire time in high school, but this time it didn't work. Needing only half an English credit to graduate, me and my laziness tried the wrong teacher and I failed.

Summer came and all my buddies were preparing for college or working, but I had nothing to do. A friend of mine wanted to go to the Navy and convinced me to join him on the buddy program. Feeling the pressure from my mother threatening to put out an eighteen-year-old jobless, school-less, young adult, I agreed to join. My friend and I took the aptitude test, which I scored high in; however, he failed and was not admitted. He was the only reason I was going in the first place, so when he no longer qualified I was no longer interested. There I was, eighteen, with absolutely nothing to do, and it was no one's fault but mine. So I made the same stupid decision so many young men with nothing to do make at that vulnerable age. I started running the streets.

Because I wasn't raised around people who were well acquainted with the street life, I had to learn and learn quickly. I was always courageous, which probably was my shield, because those who really lived that street life recognized that I didn't belong. A few people would always tell me to take my butt back to the suburbs, and every time somebody said that, it ticked me off. Especially when it came from a person I didn't like. My attitude was "try this suburban boy if you want to." I began to get into small things that led to bigger, more-complex ones, and in the span of eighteen months I was in and out of the county jail.

One evening, after coming from a neighborhood picnic in an area that I was hanging out in, a seemingly small disagreement skyrocketed into the unthinkable. The argument left one man dead. Because I was there with the shooter, I too, a young man from the suburbs with a once-bright future who chose the streets over the good sense I was raised with, was charged with his death.

It was 1996, two years after my senior year at Thornridge High School. I didn't take the long road of juvenile delinquency and group homes to get to a point where I was charged with murder. My road was a short one.

1
Animal Shelter

She was the ugliest woman I've ever seen.
Calloused, insensitive, and downright mean.
With a swelled head and swollen cheeks that housed those beady
little eyes
And two tongues in her mouth telling twice the lies.
Her speech was harsh; similar to the braying of the ass
Crass, uneducated, and devoid of class.
Vehemently she defended her children's destructive behaviors
Sons desensitized and crude
Daughters with their mother's attitude.
Defeated and depleted because their souls were so mistreated
These ignorant bastards couldn't recognize the help they needed.
Cultivated in an infected womb and nurtured so savagely
Was born an immoral generation more hideous than she!
—Yamini

I am going to begin my story with the Cook County Jail, one of the largest single-site jails in the United States. All civilized behavior ends at its barbed-wire walls. It is an animal shelter. It is as if it was created in the mind of a bestselling author of fiction. It is dangerous, volatile, and dehumanizing. I say "animal shelter" because a good number of the men here behaved like animals, county sheriffs included.

I arrived at the jail with a group of fifteen young men from all over the city, with many of us being charged with murder or attempted murder. We were mostly African Americans and Hispanics of high school and college age, and we had all just thrown our lives away. The truck pulled up to a human loading area at a back entrance of the jail and let us out. We were ushered through a large underground tunnel that connected the courthouse to the jail, stopped along a wall, and ordered to strip naked. This was the place where many infamous stories of beatings given by sheriffs took place, and on that day in September 1996, what I witnessed confirmed it.

I, along with the other men, had been in a police-station lockup for close to three days without washing and wearing the same clothing. The smell was unbearable. I remember wondering if the transatlantic slave ships smelled this bad. As I stood there naked, eight huge African American sheriffs paced up and down the line like attack dogs. Some wore face masks to cover the stench, others wore angry, disgusted frowns or contorted smirks, and all looked to steal whatever dignity any man on that wall had left.

In a loud, aggressive tone intended to intimidate, a big six-foot-two, 250-pound sheriff faced the line we were standing in and began barking orders. "Anybody with braids in their head take them out right now." I and about five others had our hair in braids and began to take them down. A young guy about my age didn't like the order and with an attitude, he slowly took his time. Seeing his dislike of the command, two huge sheriffs walked over to him, violently slapped his hands out of his hair, snatched the braids from his head, called him a couple of names, and shoved him back against the wall with tremendous force.

"Let me see your hands; fingers wide," the sheriff giving orders said. I stretched my long arms straight up and showed both sides of my hands. "Run your fingers through your hair." Now that my hair was down I combed it with my fingers to show I wasn't trying to smuggle anything into the jail. "Open your mouths wide," the big officer said. With that last command the degrading vulgarities began.

"This pretty boy got a nice-size mouth," one of the sheriffs wearing a mask said to a man standing a few feet away from me.

"She's gonna need it," another replied as they both inspected the mouth of the man they were dehumanizing. "Bend at the waist and spread them cheeks," came another order. I cringed. I couldn't stand losing my dignity, but I also knew that the cavity back there was how some people brought their drugs in with them.

When the order was given, a thin, sickly looking Hispanic man was moving too slowly. His inability to keep pace with the rest of us was obvious because of his physical condition. Just as wild predatory animals attack the lame ones among them, a sheriff outweighing this sickly, naked man by 150 pounds smashed his head against the wall with such force the crunch echoed in the tunnel. He would have collapsed had his face not been pinned between the wall and the hand of a 300-pound savage.

Completely naked and vulnerable, I angrily listened to the degrading insults. Although none of them were addressed to me, I felt like they were. I felt the other man's pain, his grief, and I was ready to fight for strangers.

In this group of sheriffs, there was a particular officer who was more vicious than the others. He was light skinned, about five foot four, and 165 pounds, and he looked like a midget compared to the ape squad. He walked up and down the line taunting our naked group for a reason beyond my understanding. He stopped in front of a guy about his size who looked weak and who didn't open his mouth wide enough when the command was given and slapped him so hard he fell into the next man. I stood there grinding my teeth so hard my jaws almost locked up.

We were told to get dressed and get back on the wall and wait for our next instructions. Once we all had our shoes and boots back on and were no longer in that vulnerable naked position, the small sheriff who stirred up the most hatred in us all was nowhere to be seen.

No one likes a coward. He is despised and rejected. It was my pride and ego's greatest challenge to witness or be subjected to abuse from the kinds of men whose hearts tremble with fear at the first sign of danger; men who will abandon you, without warning, to face a threat alone. This is what I was preparing my mind for, at least for the next few years. My terrible choices landed me here. The stupid decisions I made led me here. I chose the street life, the gutter, over my family—over everything. I was raised a God-fearing freethinker and I chose a direction that had me bending over spreading my butt cheeks to be inspected by animals. Angry and humiliated, I entered my new life with my soul on fire.

The Cook County Jail is divided into units called divisions, and in 1996 divisions one, nine, ten, and eleven were where the men with violent cases pending were housed. In the jail there were always between forty-eight and seventy-five men on one wing. The majority of them were members of one of more than ten different gangs, with many under the influence of the drug of their choice and gallons of homemade alcohol. To see so many young guys being held and facing trial for violent or heinous crimes against people was distressing. They were impulsive, without reason, devoid of logic, and living in a closet-sized space. My sane mind had a need to make sense, a need to be rational, and I was going to have to find a way to exist in this environment. But this was something I could not comprehend. This was anarchy, chaos, and like everyone else I had to survive, and it began immediately.

I was sent to division ten after the demeaning experience in the tunnel—starving, exhausted, and funky as hell. I couldn't stomach my own smell. Anyone who has been through this process knows exactly what I'm speaking of and exactly how I felt. There was nothing to be proud of. I was thinking, "What if my mother saw me standing there looking and smelling like a diseased, stray animal?" For the men who had kids, I thought, "What if your children, who adore you because they see their father as this larger-than-life figure, saw you standing there, their hero, filthy, spirit deflated, depressed, and unrecognizable?" That image of you will be burned into their minds forever.

I have never—ever seen a man come through those county doors facing charges that could get him serious time and not have that look about him. It is the stripping of dignity and the realization that I'm either going to die in this hell or leave as an old man too old to work. We were all pretrial detainees surviving and awaiting our day in court with little or no faith in beating those cases, but hoping like a mutha. That's a different kind of hope. That's an extreme hope for extreme circumstances.

I stepped through the door dragging the kind of mattress that looked like it was found in an alley against a dumpster. Lumpy and stained from God knows what, I dropped the disgusting bed roll and looked around. I saw young males in my age range, seventeen to twenty-one. Boys: thin, frail, and war-torn. Everyone looked as if his spirit had been siphoned from his body. No laughter, no good-natured conversation, no concern about the well-being of others. Nothing. Just empty shells.

The majority of these young men were smoking cigarettes, and the air in the housing unit looked like it had been blanketed from the exhaust of a raggedy car whose engine had just been started for the first time in years. They weren't smoking the stuff with filters but that "roll your own" raw tobacco that alters your skin color, blackens your lips, and will just mess you all the way up period.

The young guys had a defeated look and when they walked, their shoulders were slumped and they dragged their feet. The scene depressed me instantly. This was a school wing, and the number of young guys charged with murder and other violent crimes was higher on this one wing of males ages seventeen through twenty-one than on any other wing in division 10. The trend continued throughout all divisions in the county jail that housed men with violent offenses. The school wings were a majority of killers. This was it, my new home. Damn!

Checking out the scene that I was about to be a part of, my mind continued to race. Looking at all those young faces I thought, "Here we were, facing the aftermath of gang banging, drug dealing, and any other rebellious behavior that got us exiled from society. All pride gone, street dreams dead, relationships dead, reasoning dead, spiritually dead, and too stupid to know." Even though I was now a part of this group, I was not what they were.

Still standing in the doorway, I gathered my bed roll and walked over to the nearest phone and stared at it. What I was about to do was the worst thing I'd ever had to do in my twenty years of living. I had to call home to my mother—the woman who raised me, educated me, cultivated me, nurtured me, and placed me in an environment where I was able to develop without any abuses or influences from drugs or alcohol—to tell her I was in jail and charged with first-degree murder. I hated myself for that. I hated having to put my family through that. It was a phone call each of us had to make. I can only imagine what she went through when that news penetrated her ears and worked itself through her nervous system. I saw a picture in my mind of thousands of mothers and grandmothers on their phones when that news came through to their own ears. Can you see it?

That's what we did to them. That's how we repaid them for their sacrifices. That's how we rewarded them for all their years of love and support. Then we started whining for money.

I don't remember much about that phone call because I was numb; however, I do remember it was my youngest brother, who was in middle school at the time, who answered the phone. I don't have many blank thoughts when it comes to memorable moments, but this is one. I don't even remember the conversation. I guess the traumatic stress of it all wiped it clean from my memory. I hung up the phone, and whatever emotional roller coaster I was riding, I got off and raised my head. All eyes are always on the new guy, and he will forever be reminded of how he arrived to the wing on that first day.

Peace has no place in the county jail. It is unwelcome. The men here worship their own impulses, which were influenced by the lifestyles that led them to imprisonment.

The next morning, at 5 a.m., before I had an opportunity to find out if anyone was from my neighborhood, the deck went up. This means a wing riot. All hell had broken loose, and it is the single most dangerous time in jail or prison life. Anything can and will happen, and it usually does. Early-morning riots were not uncommon in the county jail. People were cranky and still in a swoon from their night sleep. As most of them are, this riot was caused by a young man who was a slave to his impulses.

Whatever destructive urge that this young fellow felt, he seemed to obey. I don't remember his name because I had just arrived, so I'll call him Angry.

Angry was upset because the breakfast tray he himself picked had less juice in the container than the other trays. Never mind that the juices were sealed and shipped from the manufacturer that way; never mind that it was less than an ounce difference from the seventy-five other juices. No, to hell with logic and common sense. This was an opportunity to start some mess because he was the type who enjoyed chaos. Unfortunately, so did a handful of others. This was the school wing after all, and there were no men here to talk sensibly or demand order. The only people here were overgrown little boys who, before this, were still living at home under Mama's roof.

Angry took his hard, thick plastic tray and swung it in the face of a rival gang member across the bridge of his nose. Instantly the wing exploded into violence. Fifty young men scattered around the unit, chasing each other with anything they could get their hands on. It looked like drunk, crazed soccer fans from opposite teams who hated each other storming the field with shanks, mop ringers, and broom sticks. A guy came out of his cell still half sleep and wearing shower shoes only to have his teeth knocked out with a hard object by somebody running past. It went on so long that people got tired of fighting, and when the sheriffs' response team arrived, guys were already grouped with their gangs, taking head counts and assessing the damage.

Blood was everywhere and young men were hurting. All the killer, gorilla looks were gone for the moment, and I saw the true ages of seventeen-, eighteen-, nineteen-, and twenty-year-olds. Baby faces were in tears from the pain of stab wounds, and others limped around pitifully. It was the aftermath of a medieval battle with no winners, guaranteed to happen again the moment somebody felt the impulse to kick something off.

After the wing was locked down, a lieutenant came around cell to cell to see who-all needed to go to the health care unit. Sadly, at least one-third of the people involved in the brawl had serious injuries. I already hated this place. A few days later it was business as usual on the wing, and I had a court date.

Depending on one's outlook, going to court could be an unpleasant day of dealing with riffraff and hated sheriffs or a chance to socialize and hope that you ran into people you knew who too had court dates. Every day thousands of men were ushered from their divisions to the courthouse by way of an underground tunnel. Although I traveled this tunnel a couple of nights before, the scene this morning was unexpected. I saw thousands of men, the majority African American and Hispanic, handcuffed, wearing beige uniforms, and being marshaled to judgment.

Because I wanted to get a better look at what was going on up ahead, I stood on top of an empty crate that was nearby. The scene from this vantage point sent a chill down my spine. I saw tired, depressed, defeated, handcuffed young men standing side by side as far as my eyes could see in both directions. Doom and despair were the only things present, and everyone seemed to already know his fate. We looked like slaves and the county sheriffs looked like overseers. I stepped down off of that crate and joined the rest of the prisoners, disturbed by what I just recognized. I saw slavery that day, and no one can ever convince me otherwise.

I was a new arrival to the county jail, so I had to go see the chief judge. I wasn't alone. There were a dozen others who had to do the same. I've always been observant, so when I was seated I looked around the courtroom. On one side of the room sat the accused, and on the other side of the room were ambulance-chasing, drooling lawyers. Many of them didn't have clients in the room and were there to hear who was charged with what to determine which of us needed an attorney the most. Their favorite cases involved drug dealers charged with possessing large amounts of drugs. Whenever a drug case was called, the lawyers stopped fiddling around with their notes and paid more attention to what was going on in the courtroom. That was easy money for them. However, when a serious violent crime was called, their interest was not even close. Just by looking over at the person charged with the murder or attempted murder, the attorneys quickly determined his worth and moved on. "Damn! So that's how they do it," I said to myself.

I turned my attention back to the bench where the judge was sitting when the door on the side of the courtroom opened. In walked ten lively young prosecutors conversing with one another as if they had just seen a good movie. Noticing how well dressed they were, I turned in my seat and looked at how we were dressed in comparison. They were dressed for business, while we were dressed for a soup-kitchen line. Some of us still needed showers, and our hair and beards were uncombed. Although they too were young, we were complete opposites all the way down to our skin complexions. All ten of them were white, and all fifteen or so of us were African American. But that was to be expected and was not what bothered me. What bothered me was that these young people entered the room still in conversation with one another, lined up in front of the judge's bench, received their case assignments, and left as they came, never once turning to look at us. It was business as usual and we were the business. We were nothing but case files. For the second time that morning, a chill crept down my spine. I turned to the man sitting on my right, leaned in close, and said, "We don't stand a chance."

I am not giving you my opinion on judges, state attorneys, or lawyers, because my opinions do not matter. I know of judges, state attorneys, and lawyers who truly care and truly want to make a difference, for the better, in the lives of people headed in the wrong direction. I am sharing with you my experience and what my eyes saw and ears heard, and what I felt crawling down my spine that day. Although I may not have been wise enough at the age of twenty to fully comprehend what I was seeing, I certainly understand it now that I am married with two children, an author, a public speaker, and the executive director of a nonprofit organization.

There was a two-year stretch in the jail when it seemed that judges were handing down harsher sentences than was normal. It was during this time that many men became members of faith-based groups. Muslims, Christians, Jews, Buddhists, and a few other religious organizations began to form on the wings. These religious services were already provided by the jail on their scheduled days; however, congregations grew beyond these services. Unfortunately, most of the guys joining were insincere. I had an up-close experience on how men truly believe they can deceive the one who created them by quoting scripture and appearing to be upright. Being a God-fearing man myself, I assure you this is not an attack on religion. I am just explaining to you what men did to cope with their fear because of what the judges had begun. They were gang members by day and a fellowship by evening. It was a strange mixture.

This visible insincerity made religion very unappealing to young men who didn't understand spirituality in the first place. Many of the members of these jail-wing congregations were charged with the most heinous crimes and received the harshest sentences. I recall a conversation with another prisoner on the subject, and he said, "Those stupid fools are over there playing with God and getting earthed." That's when somebody gets picked up off his feet and power-slammed to the ground face first. This sentiment was echoed throughout the jail. After seeing so many people get convicted and receive long prison sentences, I became numb to it. Life went on and I just waited for my turn.

Days, weeks, months, and years passed in this dangerous, dangerous place where nothing happened but excruciating pain. No one was ever safe and everybody knew it. That level of defenselessness had us all on edge, and we knew that the only way to survive was to be ready for anything at any time. Black Teeth, a young gang leader, had some issues in the streets with members of his own mob that spilled over into the jail. He was visiting with his family one afternoon when a couple of gangbangers from the same gang as he stormed into the visiting room and stabbed him in front of his loved ones. His young son and girlfriend saw men try to kill him, and he could do nothing but scream.

Doing time in Cook County Jail while waiting on a trial is dangerous for other reasons too. The gang infestation, of course, is the main problem, but the county sheriffs presented another. Whenever they came to restore order because of a riot, because of an individual's behavior toward another sheriff, or even because of a wing shakedown, their methods were brutal. Very often when a wing is shaken down (checked for any contraband items), a strip search is held. Sometimes sheriffs slapped, punched, kicked, and choked naked men during these shakedowns. They used gestapo tactics of intimidation and force that if caught on camera could get them all prosecuted. It was these tactics that made us despise the sheriffs.

During a surprise shakedown, a tactical team of approximately thirty men as huge as NFL players dressed in all black and wearing leather gloves burst through the wing doors. Some of them carried big sticks and were screaming loud obscenities, but all of them were extremely aggressive in their behavior. Their Rottweilers and German shepherds were almost as big as they were. As they bullied through the wing, they pushed people down and slapped others against walls. A man named Donnie wasn't moving quickly enough and he was slapped so hard that he almost lost consciousness. He was a light-skinned man, so the entire side of his face bruised instantly. In moments his eye darkened to an ugly little raisin and all the tissue around it became a swollen rainbow of dark colors. This was the tactical team's behavior all the time. The commander of the team said that this was his gang and that his gang ran the jail.

Not all county sheriffs were bad people. Some of them sincerely wanted to help, and they showed it through their kind and encouraging words. It was easy to recognize these officers, and we appreciated them. But we didn't get too close. To do so would have been dangerous for us and job threatening for them. Anyone who got too close to a county sheriff was no longer to be trusted with any information and was often mistreated on the wing, which was a dangerous situation. And the opposite was also true: any Sheriff getting too close to an inmate was ostracized by his or her peers and often placed under investigation, which could jeopardize his or her job. All of these variables created the "us against them" mentality that helped shape the thinking in the inmates and sheriffs.

Anyone who had friends and family to come and visit was considered blessed. This was a luxury and a major ingredient to remaining sane. Some men used their visits in boastful ways to show their importance. Whenever people came to see them regularly, they made it appear that they had status in their neighborhoods. Fat Sean had this bad. He was a small-time neighborhood drug dealer who loved to flash every little bit of anything. Every time he got a visit he would go into an "I'm sick of feeding these cats from my cell" kind of spiel like he really had it like that. Another guy, Caddy, would put on cologne just to go out into the visiting room and talk to his visitor through a thick glass with a tightly wired mouthpiece to speak through. There were no contact visits in the county jail, so watching him prepare on a weekly basis was ridiculous. Those who didn't receive many visits, if any, had a hard time surviving and were forced to make it off of the few rations provided by the jail.

Time in the county jail is torture. I must repeat myself over and over and over again, because the day-to-day threat was real. Life there was as unpredictable as a tornado's path, and it made men take plea deals from state's attorneys just to escape the madness. A riot once erupted because somebody changed the channel from a kids show to the news. Two young guys who were watching Power Rangers jumped up and cussed out the man who changed the channel, calling him all kinds of names. He slapped one of them and all hell broke loose.

What's absolutely insane about the majority of these explosions is that right before they ignite, men in rival gangs may be sitting with each other playing cards or board games. But because they are in rival gangs, the moment a situation escalates, they attack one another only to later apologize, saying, "You know how this thang go."

During the riot, a Hispanic man named Los was knocked unconscious and had to be taken to the healthcare unit. He had been in the county jail for close to a year, and up until that time he had not been involved in or victimized by the stupid, senseless, random violence. A few days after his recovery, Los called his attorney, had him get his court date moved up, went before his judge, and made a plea deal for five years. This was a recurring trend in this treacherous place, and no one was laughed at or made fun of when he went to court and took a plea deal to get the hell out of that animal shelter.

After the riot, the sheriffs rounded up everyone who was seen fighting. When these brawls go down, they are chaotic frenzies, and it is very difficult to distinguish friend from foe. I was in the dayroom on the phone when it happened, so I dropped the reciever and put my back to a wall, swinging at whoever got too close, trying my best not to take out people I became friends with. After the brawl, the sheriffs rounded up people to take to segregation, but because the fight was so large it was impossible to take everyone involved. Only a handful were grabbed, and unfortunately for me I was one of them.

Segregation, or "seg" as we called it, is an isolated place in the county jail where people are sent who violate the rules and regulations established for maintaining order. It is twenty-four-hour lockdown and is usually filled with men who have been involved in brutal fights, stabbings, assaults on sheriffs, possession of drugs or hooch, and other acts detrimental to safety and security. It is intended to be a dark, lonely place, but because the jail has so much rebellious behavior, segregation was just another wing. Looking around, my first reaction was, "This ain't as bad as the sheriffs made it out to be." Guys were going to seg intentionally just to meet up with their buddies, and when I arrived I was familiar with a majority of the people there. It was a hang-out spot.

While I was in segregation, I sang, rapped, told yo-mama jokes, and clowned other people just like everybody else. One afternoon as the dinner trays were being collected it was determined by the shift commander that the wing was to be split up because people were having too good a time. Two-man cells were made into one-man cells, and anyone with only a few days left to complete his segregation term was released back into the general population. The area where I was located was the noisiest, and the split-up began there.

As the rearranging began, I voiced my displeasure to the sheriffs about them breaking up our little corner and explained that all we were trying to do was kick it. At twenty-two years old, immature and under the influence of my environment, I got caught up in the moment and ran my mouth, telling the officers how bogus they were as they arrived to my cell. Yeah, I told 'em real good. I laid the G down and continued talking crazy as I was ordered to move into one of the cells nearest to the hub where the sheriffs surveyed the entire wing.

I grabbed my property and walked toward the front of the segregation unit. "This is your cell r-i-g-h-t h-e-r-e," the officer said in a sinister, ominous tone. When I walked into the cell, I knew immediately I had crossed the threshold into a deeper, darker dimension of the criminally insane. Judging by the layout of this chamber, I could easily tell that the man inside of it was used to living alone.

Taking a few more steps into the cell and looking around in disbelief, I was shocked by what I saw. Cut-out photos of women from pornography magazines covered the walls like wallpaper. On the table was a small shrine of more naked books dedicated to his perversion, but leaning against the pile was a figure of a woman made from the magazine pages. I was getting creeped out.

I knew many men who had a naked book or two, or three or four, but this was without a doubt the most extreme case I've ever seen. Resisting the urge to turn around and bang on the cell door for somebody to get me the hell out of there, I dragged my property over to the bunk and looked down in more disbelief.

Lying on the mattress was yet still more sexually explicit material. "My bad, celly [cellmate], let me get that for you. I ain't used to living with nobody," said a short, thin person who looked to be suffering from malnutrition. Standing there slowly turning my body around the cell to take it all in, I said, "I see."

In the corner, on the opposite side of the cell, were stacks of court papers and case documents that came up to the waist of my 6-foot-4 build. People who were very active in fighting their cases along side their attorneys often had a lot of paper work but nothing like this. Stacks like these had to take years and years to compile. Shrugging it off and unpacking the few items I had I tried to get settled in but I was too uneasy about this entire situation. Those mounds of documents in the corner were just as bizarre as the porn and for some reason it was bothering the hell out of me. Curious, but not wanting to talk much I pulled out a Tom Clancy book I was reading and knocked out a few chapters before I dozed off.

Later that evening I was awakened to what sounded like loud whispering. I sat up in my bunk and scanned the cell to see if an officer had come in and was having a conversation with my celly. Finding no one there, I slowly leaned forward and peeked over the side of the top bunk and saw Ol' Boy having a full-blown argument with a naked centerfold he had torn from one of his magazines. "You all right down there, celly?" I asked, startling him.

He looked up at me and said, "My bad, celly, didn't mean to wake you. Just checkin' one of my hoes."

"Yeah, a pimp got to do that sometimes," I said, going along with the situation. In complete and utter disbelief, I rolled over and stared at the ceiling. "This is what I get for acting a damn fool," I told myself. It was the last time I woofed at anyone.

I was so disturbed by my surroundings that I stayed up all night and didn't nod off until around 4 a.m. A few hours later I woke to the sound of heavy movements in the cell. Ol' Boy was packing up all his property and moving to another cell where he could be alone again.

The next morning eight huge tact team officers the size of defensive linemen came on the seg unit and waited by Ol' Boy's door as he got dressed for court. They were there to escort him through the jail and into the courtroom because of his high profile case. As it turned out, Ol' Boy was facing charges for several rapes and murders of women on Chicago's south side.

Because I chose to run my mouth to the sheriffs as if I had some authority to do anything, I was tossed in a cell with a person charged with being a serial killer. Nothing about his appearance was threatening, nor did I feel threatened. I was at least 6 inches taller and 50 pounds heavier, and I could handle myself well. I was, however, almost traumatized by what I experienced. I'm still weirded out by that one night in the realm of the psychotic.

A few weeks went by and more and more people left seg to return to the general population. The party was over, and the disciplinary unit became the dreary place it was designed to be. There were only four of us left to finish our segregation time in a place that could house close to fifty men. The silence was so unnatural it felt like all of the sound that was recently there had been sucked out by the huge air vents that hung from the ceiling. It was so quiet I heard the office phone whenever it rang through thick, bulletproof glass and layers of reinforced steel doors and concrete walls.

The four of us who remained after everyone else had gone were Ol' Boy, a psychopathic rapist and murderer; a middle-aged Hispanic man who barely spoke a lick of English; a short, powerfully built, hell-raising deaf man; and me. I had no intention of ever saying a word to Ol' Boy or the deaf guy because they were lunatics, and communicating with the Hispanic man was impossible. So there I was, stuck in seg with all the books I took with me already read, no cellmate, no one to talk to, no food, and two weeks left to do. It was just me, my puzzle books, my deck of cards, and my imagination. I thought back to what a sheriff told me about seg when I first arrived.

"You gon' feel it when the party's over," he said. He wasn't lying. I was dying of boredom and from the lack of human companionship. I couldn't take it. The hours felt like days. I never knew exactly what time it was, only that it was morning, afternoon, evening, or night. To keep from losing my mind, I read my books over again. By default, The Hunt for Red October became my favorite book.

After my segregation time ended I went back to population and found that some of the gangs were trying to get a handle on their members because the violence had gotten to be too much, even by their standards. To get order meant brutal violations for anyone putting the rest of the mob in danger, but those violations were so ruthless that they did more harm than good. Some of the gang leaders were so drunk with power that they were the biggest threat to their group. It was a control issue. Because it was too dangerous to start trouble with opposing gangs, many started trouble among their own, and when it happened it was vicious. The members knew that their gang leaders would stomp their ears together if they caught them doing anything outside of the mob's rules, but some members were so rebellious that they did things anyway. For their own protection from the backlash, they would ask the sheriffs if they could be placed in protective custody forever, marking them as cowardly to the rest of the population.

Most gangs cooperated in an allied system that was designed by the gang leaders. When it comes time for war, gangs, like countries, come together to form a bigger group. The opposing group also has alliances with other gangs to become a unit just as big. This was why the riots were so huge. Although each gang is independent on its own, whenever violence erupts, an allied member is expected to assist his ally.

In the county jail, whenever prisoners moved from one place to another, such as from the cell house to the gym, the potential for chaos was real. To keep the chances of an explosion of violence as low as possible, the gangs were separated from each other by being placed on the opposite ends of the line. If someone from a rival gang would be standing in part of the line reserved for the rival mob, a serious fight could break out, and many times, it did.

In the middle of the line, serving as a barrier between the two groups, was the place for all the neutrons (non-gang-affiliated people). Neutrons had it bad, especially when they were white men. It was payback time, and white inmates in Cook County Jail were punching bags. They were bullied, beaten, and extorted. It was sad to see young African Americans and Latinos become abusive, mean-spirited, savage bullies just because there was an opportunity for some get-back. Many of these young gang members who treated white men so savagely weren't even racist. It was just some bully stuff. I was glad that most inmates didn't treat those men like that. But when it did happen, it was bad.

There were not a lot of white inmates in lockup. The majority of them bonded out. They weren't given the excessive bonds that African Americans and Latinos were getting from judges, nor were they as poor. There was no way their families were going to leave them in a place where they could be severely harmed on a day-to-day basis as long as there was a way to get them out of custody.

In division ten, where I was housed, there was no laundry service. I will say it again: there was no laundry service. I had to do my laundry in one of three ways: (1) get an empty mop bucket, (2) get a trash bag, or (3) use the sink in my cell. I used the mop bucket the most often. I put as much water in it as I needed, asked around for state soap (small motel like bars provided by the jail), and then washed my clothes. The trash-bag method works similar to the washing machine. Simply fill it up and shake like hell until your arms get tired. Repeat the process several times and it might work. The sink was also a common method. The problem was that the sink bowl was so small, it was difficult to put much in it. Some people would even wash their clothes in the toilet. This was mostly done by newcomers who would do their laundry without asking how it's done.

Sometimes the mop bucket and trash bags were not available, sometimes the wing was out of bags, and sometimes we had to deal with officers who wouldn't unlock the utility closets where all the cleaning supplies were kept. What added to the frustration of doing laundry was that the jail made no effort to provide us with means to do so. Whenever people decided to wash their underclothes and Department of Corrections (DOC) uniforms on the same day, clothes would be hanging all over the wing; homemade clotheslines would be everywhere. That meant tearing a sheet into strips and then tying the ends once it was long enough to do what you needed. The problem was that it was against the rules.

Many times, when a sheriff came on the wing to take count during shift changes, he/she would cut the clotheslines down and throw them in the garbage, leaving our freshly cleaned laundry lying on a dirty jail floor. This is how some of the officers treated us. Many of them flat out didn't care that there were necessities that we didn't have, and when we tried to improvise they were callous and cold about it, saying rules are the rules. Having to deal with these people made life more frustrating than it already was. On one hand, the environment was treacherous and unpredictable, and on the other hand, a good many of the authorities were what we called "cranks."

The Cook County Jail is a dangerous, nonproductive, volatile, dehumanizing, and sanity-threatening place. There is no growth there. It is the gateway to the penitentiary, and there is no escaping its experience if you are ever charged with a felonious offense.

After three years and two months of waiting my trial began and ended with such speed it is still difficult remembering everything that happened. I faced my judgment during a period when judges were slamming people hard. The sentences being handed down were so excessive they may as well have been life. Anyone charged with murder or attempted murder and chose a jury and lost might never see the world again. For what seemed like three of the longest years in human history, I sat and watched young African American men my age facing similar and even less-severe charges get hit with so much time it scared people to death and made them take plea deals.

Right before my trial began, Li'l Rock, a twenty-two-year-old African American man I had known my entire county stay, had just returned from his sentencing hearing. Judging by the look on his face I asked him, "Do I wanna know?"

With the cracking voice of a dying boy he said, "By the time I come home the Bible gon' have a newer testament."

"Damn," I said and walked away.

I knew not to play with these judges. Although I had no intention of copping out, I did make the decision, without council, to take a bench trial. My attorney was an overworked public defender with a bunch of other cases. I had little faith in him. Like everyone I knew in the Cook County Jail with the same type of case, I was found guilty of first-degree murder under the theory of accountability and sentenced to thirty years in the Illinois Department of Corrections, of which I was to serve half.

2

You Home Now Boy

With difficulty comes ease

Or it was supposed to be

The ball was in our possession

And like a running back with two left hands, it was fumbled

From the sidelines I watched my people scramble

For the hope that took a lifetime to achieve

And like the perfect woman it eluded the arms of every man that

fell upon it

Then the floods came

The outside observers grew impatient with the performance of a

team that should have improved and made their way towards the

exits

Unwanted burdens fell from clouds that were as dark as Satan's

suggestions

The coaches dropped their heads in disappointment

Fights broke out between teammates

The prima donnas against the blue collars

Misguided cheerleaders rooting on the fight instead of the game

It was such a shame

Real pain

*Owners and officials met in secret to keep this cancer from
spreading to the rest of the league*
*The commissioner said sedate them and shower them with
abundant gifts*
Before anyone amongst this group regains his consciousness!
—*Yamini*

In the Department of Corrections, whether the Illinois DOC
(IDOC) or Cook County DOC, there was the problem of
population control. Sometimes men were held in the jail for
weeks after they had been convicted and sentenced because there
was absolutely no place to house them in the penal institutions. I
knew a handful of men who were still in the county for weeks
after their trials. Over the years this problem reached a critical
stage, but in 1999, when I was convicted and sent to the
penitentiary, my transferal took a total of five days.

The bus ride was one I'll never forget because it was the last
look at the free world that I got for a long time. I was on my way
to a prison whose primary function was the intake of convicted
men for processing so that we could be shipped to the designated
penitentiaries where we were to serve our sentences. The ride
was a quiet one, each man to his own thoughts. I could think of
nothing more than how much I disappointed my family, even
though I had spent the previous three years in the county jail

thinking it. I carried that burden for years, and it wasn't until the latter part of my sentence that I recognized God had forgiven me and had mercy on me, which enabled me to forgive myself.

When we arrived in Joliet, the prison looked like an old battle-worn eighth-century outpost on its last legs, ready to crumble during the next thunderstorm. After stopping inside the main gate, all of the prisoners were ushered off the bus in shackles into a small gym next to the health-care unit. Here we had to strip naked for search, dress in the prison gear, and visit the nurse practitioner for medical documentation. This process alone seemed to take ten hours.

Buses were arriving from every county jail and lockup in the northern half of the state. The arrivals and departures were nonstop, and I thought, "This is big business. This place is as busy as an airport." One by one, thousands of men were processed into the state penal system, where we lost our names and were given numbers that would identify us as long as we were in custody in the IDOC. Yeah, we lost our names. My dignified name, Yamini, which means the right hand, became unimportant compared to my ID number.

After the processing and probing from the health-care administrators, each group was led to the chow hall for dinner. When I entered the building, I noticed right off the bat that there was a target board hanging from the ceiling about thirty feet directly in front of the gun tower. It was used for warning shots to cease unruly behavior from prisoners, and the surface of it was completely dented from hundreds of buckshot rounds. The condition of it told the story of what sometimes happens in this place without anyone ever having to ask.

Standing in line waiting to eat, I was handed a tray with an amount of food that may have been sufficient for an eight-year-old, but not a grown man. I was really hungry and the food portion on my tray was smaller than other people's, or at least it seemed so. I asked the food supervisor for a little more, and his reply was one that I kept with me my entire prison sentence. He said, "My job is not to get you full but to keep you alive."

The dinner menu often determines the size of the crowd that comes out to eat. Chicken, hamburgers and fries, and pizza were the common draws to make people come out to the chow hall, and the large crowd would cause long delays. The delays made most people regret ever coming out, especially if the weather conditions were poor. However, the thing I disliked most about the chow hall was the lack of time that we were given to eat our meals.

Eating in the chow hall was so aggravating that many men developed bad attitudes from this experience alone. A person could have been having a not so terrible day until he went out to eat and had to deal with the behavior of the guards there. Some correctional officers enjoyed watching us wolf down our food and made a game of it, whereas others put people out for not moving quickly enough.

After dinner I was escorted to the cell house with my group, where we would remain until our transportation arrived to take us to our designated penitentiaries. Depending on the bed space available at that prison, this wait could take days or weeks. To wait weeks was the worst-case scenario, and it meant that you had to sit alone in a cell with no property, books, or magazines. Nothing. Just you and your thoughts. If you were lucky the prison guard might let you read his newspaper.

I stayed in the intake prison for five days before the bus arrived that I was to leave on. That morning after breakfast I was given an indigent bag that had a few personal-hygiene items so that I could take a shower, because I hadn't had one since I left the county jail. Written on the bag were a letter and a number that indicated what prison I was going to be transferred to. I asked officers and porters (inmate janitors) about the number on my bag and where I was being shipped to, and they all gave me the same answer. They said that I was heading to a minimum-security facility. Immediately, I thought that was a mistake. The nature of the offense that I was convicted of didn't allow inmates into that kind of lower level prison without first being housed in a penitentiary with higher security status to determine their aggression level. It just didn't add up.

I gave my paperwork to an officer to check into it for me without giving him any additional information that would make him aware that I wasn't supposed to be going to a low-level prison. He came back with the same answer I had already been given—minimum security. What? I couldn't believe it. I was so happy I thanked God like I had never thanked Him before. I was so relieved for being spared a traumatic experience that my eyes watered.

The ride on the bus was as numbing as the ride when I left the county jail. It was silent. The only sound was the rubber from the wheels on the road and the clanking of shackles and chains every time we hit a bump. Damn.

The demeanor of the correctional officers who were responsible for our transport was easy-going. Each of them was middle-aged and each had been working for the Department of Corrections for at least twenty-five years. Their behavior and speech showed sympathy for what we were about to go through; however, this was about to change.

After a few hours, our bus arrived at a prison that had open gates, small bungalows, and streets that looked like neighborhoods. "This doesn't look so menacing," I thought. We sat in the parking lot for twenty minutes when all of a sudden, empty buses began to arrive. As it turned out, this penitentiary served as a drop-off point for buses from the northern region of the state, and only a couple of people got off because they were assigned to that prison.

A few more minutes passed before a lieutenant from one of the buses that just pulled up climbed onto our bus and began to read a list of ID numbers. He instructed all the men whose numbers were just read to get up, come forward, and exit the bus. The names and numbers on his list were all headed to maximum security.

When he got to the bottom of his list, the lieutenant repeated the ID number of someone who didn't answer. He repeated it again, but still, no answer. A few of the prisoners began making jokes about somebody being so scared to go to a max joint he won't get his butt off the bus. Holding a file in his hand with a photocopy of someone's face, the lieutenant slowly walked down the aisle looking for the man in the photo. When he stopped he was standing right over me, making sure the picture in his hand was the person he was standing in front of. He looked at me and said, "Are you Omar Yamini, K78270?" Shocked that he said my name, my mind began racing as to why. I was told by people who I thought were giving me accurate information that I was being transferred to a minimum-security prison. S-u-c-k-e-r. In a prison environment that is operated by both officers and inmates, I was square as a pool table and twice as green. Part of me knew that I had no business going to a minimum-security prison after being convicted of first-degree murder, but the other part was hoping like hell that it was true.

When I got up from my seat, the clowning began. "Boo," somebody yelled. "Ain't no need in being scared, big fella," somebody else said. "That must've been him back here smellin' like that" and "Better check them draws" were others. Shamed and embarrassed I made my way to the front of the bus and was actually glad to be leaving it.

"Are you gon' be a problem?" the lieutenant asked me. "I called you four times."

"Naw, no problem," I said. "You were reading ID numbers and I've never been called by an ID number before. I don't even know the damn thing yet."

"Fair enough," he said, and that was the end of it. I boarded the bus that was headed to maximum security for what seemed like a thirty-hour ride.

I've had my share of dramatic experiences in my life, but what happened next will stay with me forever. Night had fallen as we got close to the maximum-security prison. The bus turned down a dark road surrounded by tall, thick trees. Whatever twilight was left in the sky was suffocated the moment we made that turn. The lights on the bus went off immediately, as if the driver was intentionally adding to the effect of an already strange scene. Then he picked up speed. The engine raced and the tires barely held onto the pavement as the driver leaned into curves. I'm thinking this man must have been down this road a thousand times, because ain't no way in hell anybody unfamiliar with it would drive in such pitch blackness so recklessly.

Any prisoner who was sleep was now awake, and we all were trying to figure out what was going on. Everything about what was happening was bizarre. Thoughts entered my head about the history of this southern part of the state, and an ambush was on my mind. But before I could finish entertaining the thought, we burst through an opening that was lit like a night game at a football stadium. Menard, big, wicked, foul, Castle Grayskull-looking monstrosity appeared on our left. For any of you who are not familiar with Castle Grayskull, it is the home of an evil, sinister character in the He-Man cartoon I grew up watching.

Menard's walls looked like they stretched at least a quarter mile in each direction. Razor-sharp barbed wire covered rows and rows of chained-link fences that ran the length of the walls. Gun towers, no, outposts, were on top of the walls every fifty yards. An enormous steel door that looked like it could be the entrance to a 747 airplane hangar had bolts the size of my shoes bulging from it. I could hear the gears turning, clanking, and screeching as it opened like a mouth ready to swallow food. My life flashed before my eyes. I said, "Oh my God, what have I done? What have I done that I have to go in there?"

If this sounds like a fictitious story, believe me, it is not. This was real. I am sharing with you what these eyes saw when I arrived at a maximum-security prison for the first time in my life. All movies, all TV shows, all descriptions from any person who has ever been to prison meant absolutely nothing to me. Nothing in my life prepared me for this scene, and judging by the look on some of the young men's faces my age, they were just as dizzy and nauseated as I was.

To say this was shocking is not stating it correctly. This was an electrocution. I may as well have been pinned down by a rancher's boot and maliciously cattle-prodded. Nothing in my memory or understanding could help me calm my nervous system. Prison was not the fear I knew of. Although some men had it, prison is not the trembling, "what's that noise; somebody's going to hurt me" fear. It's the fear of being kept, treated, and controlled like an animal; the fear of losing your human dignity.

We didn't all make it. On the bus ride we had a few guys making a lot of noise and talking nonsense, but when we got to the gates of hell, a big dude with the biggest mouth had a nervous breakdown. When he saw this maximum-security penitentiary he freaked, hyperventilated, and all other kinds of panic-related stuff. I thought he was going to faint and pass out. When it was time for us to exit the bus, he clung to his seat like an infant to his mother. The officers rushed on to pull him off and one of them told him, "Quit your whining. You home now, boy."

Castle Grayskull, this monstrosity of a prison, was on my left, but on my right were train tracks with at least fifteen prison guards with riot pumps, shotguns, and huge four-legged beasts. Behind these correctional officers was the mighty Mississippi River, and it was flowing; I could see how powerful it really was. Handcuffed and chained to each other, we moved slowly toward the open door. I hate handcuffs and chains. It has a strange effect on me. My mind goes to slavery and the transatlantic slave trade, and that's where I was at that moment, looking at all those prison guards with those weapons—they were all white men.

In my group there were a couple Hispanics and a couple Caucasians, but we African American men were the overwhelming majority, and we were in chains, moving very slowly, overseen by armed white men with dogs standing on train tracks with a river flowing behind. That was the scene. What I witnessed that day was a scene I've always imagined straight out of the South during slavery. It was eerie; it was weird; it was creepy. In a low growl more to myself than to

others I mumbled, "You mutha f——. You m-u-t-h-a f——."
The connection to me was clear. Some masterminds found a way
to do this legally.

For the second time I entered a penal institution on fire.
Needing to calm down, I slowly walked into the prison and
looked around. What I saw was a small community; a mini-
settlement that looked like a combination of a Wild West town
and a medieval village sitting against a steep, rocky hillside. The
walls looked like they served as protection from outside forces,
only many of the structure's convicted inhabitants were cruel,
vicious men banished here forever. I was no longer in the world I
knew.

Trying hard to recover from the shock, I was led to the chapel
for strip search. Yes, the chapel, where we were stripped of
clothing and had our body cavities searched, in a house of
worship. A strip search to me is and will always be one of the
most demeaning things a person can go through. As in the
county jail, I was instructed to strip completely naked, open my
mouth, run my fingers through my hair, lift up my scrotal sac,
bend at the waist, and spread my butt cheeks. God I hated this.
Hated it, hated it, hated it. Do you have any idea what it's like
for someone to stand in front of you and demand that you bend
over and spread your butt cheeks?

After the strip search we were led to a receiving area where we had to live for a few days before we were admitted to the general prison population. For many penitentiaries this is procedure, so bed space can be found and a review of a new prisoner's medical history can be made. When I walked into the cell, I couldn't believe that I was about to be held there. This ridiculousness just didn't stop. It was so small that I could literally touch the walls fingertip to fingertip, and two large adult men had to share its submarine like quarters. With the sink, toilet, and bunk bed packed in, it was so narrow that my celly and I could not move around at the same time. I have been in bathrooms in small homes bigger than this. This cell was the size of a storage closet. "Is this legal?" I asked my new cellmate. This was a cage where you put an animal. If the sink, toilet, and bunk bed were removed, it would have been just enough room for a dog to walk in circles.

The proper perception of a prison cell is a cage. Please understand that. Every time I entered or exited it, a heavy steel door slammed shut and was locked by a steel key that looked to be 10 inches long and a quarter of an inch thick.

As if the small size of my new cage wasn't inhuman enough, it was also a bathroom. The toilet was literally two feet away from everything. Whenever my celly sat down and took a dump, I had to smell him. I had to smell his filth and he had to smell mine. The only thing I could do was move a couple of feet over and turn my back to give him the most privacy that I possibly could. That was his private space; me turning my back so my peripheral vision wouldn't pick him up when he had his pants down around his ankles handling his business. Many times the entire cell house smelled like a garbage dump, like a zoo. The smell was so nauseating it couldn't be adjusted to.

Every morning when the first shift came on to work, the steel bars on the cell doors were tested to see if any of them were loose. A loose bar meant someone was trying to escape or make a deadly weapon. This test required an officer to whack every single bar on the front of the cell with another steel rod. It was so loud it could wake the dead, and that's exactly what it did. Have you ever been in a good sleep and someone intentionally clangs something so loudly by your ear that you are shocked into consciousness? That's what this was.

I'll never forget the first time this bar rapping woke me up. I was traumatized and disoriented. I had no idea who or where I was, and after the stunned daze wore off I saw a short, overweight, middle-aged man standing in front of my cell and dragging a pipe across the bars: CLANG, CLANG, CLANG, CLANG, CLANG, CLANG, CLANG, CLANG, CLANG. It was torture on my ears. There was no adapting to this anguish; no way of adjusting to the agony of a loud, unexpected explosion of sound. I just wanted it to stop, so I pressed my hands against my ears using the kind of pressure needed to stop the bleeding of a gaping wound.

When the shock wore off, I was fuming. It was 7:30 a.m., a new day, and I was completely heated, which in prison is not a good thing. Starting a day off on the wrong foot had a tendency to get ugly, and an ugly day in the penitentiary could be bloody or an extension to your sentence. Once the sleep, the only place many men can find true peace, was violently disturbed by harsh noise, it was hard for some prisoners to restore any calm. What frustrated me was that judging by the look on some of the guards' faces, they were enjoying every moment of it. I learned to wake up just before shift change so that I wouldn't be blasted from slumber by a practice that to me seemed intended to aggravate. This was my arrival. This was how I was introduced to the penitentiary.

Once my brief stay in receiving was done, I was moved to a housing unit that was called the gladiator dome. It was called that because most of the fights, stabbings, and brawls that happened in the prison went down in that cell house. It was also the place where people were sent with disciplinary issues, or those deemed to be high security risks. There were more men in this cell house sentenced to natural life and other triple digits than any other housing unit in the prison. A good number of them had been dead for years, had lost all human sensitivity, and seemed to be completely unaffected by anything that was happening around them. To watch men transform into this type of creature was horrifying. Not all of them were going to die here; the lifers were not the only ones who lost their sensitivities.

As a child I went to the zoo a lot with my family, and one of my favorite places was the ape house. Walking up to the so-called "gladiator dome," I recognized the design immediately. "Well I'll be damned," I said. It looked like someone had taken the ape house design and used it to design the penitentiary cell house. When I walked through the door and looked up, all I could see was rows and rows of cells. There were five floors, called galleries, that reached the roof of the building, and on each gallery was a row of twenty-five cells that housed two men each. Each cell was like an exhibit, and in each exhibit were two people who were kept like animals.

Cell after cell, men were sitting idle doing nothing, staring at their TVs, or pacing the few available feet, or balled up under sheets waiting to die or for their sentences to end. When I came to my cell, my new celly was doing exactly what everyone else was doing in the twenty-five cells I passed by—staring at his TV. He didn't even get up. I went in, set my property down, and started arranging my personal items as homely as possible while being mindful that I had to share this tiny space.

My new cellmate, Bumba, was a short, middle-aged man from the Caribbean with a serious pot belly due to a refusal to exercise. Every time yard or gym was called, he lay there with his hands folded, resting them on his mound of a stomach and staring at his TV screen. He didn't need a TV guide because he was one. Whenever anybody wanted to know when a show came on and what channel, they just called down to him. Bumba was so addicted to television that he would turn it on in the middle of the night while he used the toilet, only to turn if off again when he was done. He was also a chain smoker's chain smoker who smoked a box of tops roll-up tobacco a day. I couldn't take the smoke, so I spent a lot of time sitting at the front of the cell with my face pressed between the bars.

Many times there were tours given to people who were interested in prisons for whatever reason, and they would come through escorted by prison guards in groups. Sometimes they were all white, and sometimes they were all Asian. They would walk down the galleries while we were in our cages, looking and observing the surroundings. It was times like those that I really felt like I was on display. It made my skin crawl and spine tingle because those people looked at us like we were property, like real estate.

I wasn't in the cell house forty-eight hours before the first group came through. At first I thought they were human rights activists, and then I got rid of that idea because they never spoke to any of us or showed any concern for our well-being; they were just looking, pointing, and taking mental notes. I had no idea what their business was, but because I learned to obey my senses, everything about it felt very sinister and I could feel it in my soul.

The next day I went out to the yard for the first time in a maximum-security prison, and my entire life and future were put into perspective. This was a new experience for me, and there were easily four hundred people out there, half of whom, if not more, would likely die here. As I was thinking this, Crash, someone I spent three years with in the Cook County jail, called my name like he was happy to see me. He was sentenced to 850 years.

Crash and I were walking around the yard, him giving me the layout of the joint, when Troll, another young man I knew from the county, joined us. Troll had been sentenced to two consecutive life sentences, and the only thing that came to my mind was, "I'm walking with the dead. I am walking around this exercise track with two men who are going to die in prison." I had been sentenced to thirty years, of which I had to do half. Of that half, three were already spent in the county jail, so my prison sentence was going to be a total of twelve more years.

Walking with these two guys, whom I liked because they were good guys but were under the harmful influence of a gang-infested home life, made me change the way I was going to deal with prison. I had a light at the end of my tunnel that suddenly was getting brighter and brighter, and it was at that very moment that I had no more complaints about when I was getting out or how much time I had left to do. It was at that time I started making preparations for my future. I was going to have an opportunity to come home and start a family. I was going to have the opportunity to pursue an education and any of the ambitious goals that I set for myself. I knew that I was coming home thirty-five years old, in the middle of my prime, and able to contribute to my family and community.

Talking to men with boatloads of time was one of the most depressing things I had to go through. Some of them, even though they had been convicted and slapped with "Star Trek" time, turned out to be good men.

The prison yard was huge. It was as big as a stadium, and when the weather was nice the entire cell house might be out. All the gangs in the joint are out there on the yard, and each of them has "security duties." When I say "security duties," I'm telling you that there are pairs of men posted at certain areas or roaming the yard or the track, or standing by the basketball courts or the weightlifting area where the weightlifting equipment is kept.

They appear to be just hanging around, but they are keeping a watch so that nothing happens to any of their members.

Once, a friend of mine got in trouble with his gang and his penalty was a fine and extra security duty. He accepted the penalty over the alternative, a violation, which would have gotten him beat damn near to death. He was on security for thirty days, and every time we came outside to yard or went to the gym he had to spend his leisure time standing around watching others. I pitied him because not only was he "treated"(picked on) by his mob, but he also used to do things like "gambling off ass" (gambling with no money), leaving his gang members to have to pay the bill if he lost. He ended up checking himself in protective custody for one of these gambling stunts because he knew that his next violation was going to send him to the intensive care unit.

Sometimes whoever is on security may be watching over a particular member of his gang, someone with some authority, or "juice" as it was called. A man with authority would have some sucker on his "personal security," a bodyguard following him around the prison everywhere he went. It was a spectacle. To see men following the movements of other prisoners like they were rulers, protecting them from all harm, was something unbelievable.

I once asked a guy I knew who was on the personal security of one of the so-called gang chiefs how he got that assignment. "Did you volunteer; did you want to be the one to keep him safe?" I asked him. Before he could answer I added, "You made it. If moms could see you now!" That was my way of making him aware of how stupid what he was doing was, and how ridiculous he looked doing it.

The soldiers, as they were called, were young men who have no authority in the gang and were often the ones standing around making sure everything was cool. They either carried a weapon on them or had one nearby. The weapon was something they made, some type of shank or sharp, skin-piercing piece of anything that they got from somewhere. It didn't matter what it was as long as it had the potential to do serious damage. These were called the sendoff men. Here they were, standing around outside with handcrafted weapons that, if they got caught with them in their possession, could get them a year segregation time and charged with a crime. Also, depending on the weapon's number of inches determined how much time they received.

Many of these young men were abused by the leadership of their gangs. Smoke, another young guy I knew, was accused of "slackin'on s" (security) by his gang and was put in a full-nelson by one of his mob's biggest and strongest goons. He couldn't move an inch and could only squirm when he got his "head to toe" beat down. There was so much blood after the cruel, inhumane attack that the area was sealed off by what looked like a hazmat team.

Getting adjusted to penitentiary living, I had to deal with one extreme after another. The first time I went to religious services added to the twisted reality of this lifestyle. The services were held in an old auditorium but were sectioned off so that different denominations of the same faith would have their own area to hold their meetings. The layout was odd. Men were hating on each other's groups so hard that the prisoners in population called them religious gangbangers, and it opened the door for internal affairs to come in and add further aggravation.

In what appeared to me to be an attempt to discourage people from coming to religious services, internal affairs officers began setting up cameras wherever a group congregated and recorded its meetings. Everyone who considered himself a part of that faith was documented. Their behaviors, comments, ideas, and religious ideologies were all recorded, and sometimes, when a person would speak, the internal affairs officer holding the camera would turn in his direction and move in a little closer to the speaker. It was so irritating that it could be assumed that their purpose was to intentionally aggravate people to get a violent reaction from them. Any response like that would get the service canceled and the group labeled as a security threat group.

Other services were closely watched for different reasons, because the chapel was also the place where stolen merchandise was sold. It was the black market. Clothing items from the clothing room, food from commissary, cleaning equipment from the storage rooms—anything people could get their hands on from their assignments was pushed in what was supposed to be a house of worship. Because everybody knew what was going on, including the guards, it made the religious services a place under heavy security, and for that reason no one wanted to be there.

Of all the things that were going on in the chapel, the biggest reason religious service was closely watched was the low-down, immoral, shameful debauchery going down in there. The prostitutes would come to service to turn tricks. They would sit off to the side, either trying to catch someone's attention or waiting for someone they had set up a meeting with.

I once saw two of them scanning the room, hoping someone was interested. Of course, as they always do, they found somebody wanting to turn a trick. This was their hustle and they had absolutely no shame in their game. When the prostitute found his trick, the two of them went around the corner, out of sight to the bathroom, while the trick's buddy remained in his seat to be the lookout. A couple of moments later, guards rushed into the bathroom, caught them in the act, came out laughing at what they had seen, and told everybody what was going down. They didn't have any shame either.

Being exposed to this sick, strange new world was more than just a culture shock to me. It was a fight within to not accept the madness that had become normal behavior for the people living and working here. I had been witnessing behaviors that were hard for me to comprehend, and though there were some things I was adjusting to, the first time I ever took a shower in a maximum-security prison I was reminded of the brutality that could happen at any time.

Showers in this maximum-security prison were treated like privileges. No matter how funky or foul smelling our bodies became, we were only given three showers a week. All other bathing was done in the sinks of our cells with our celly two feet away. The officer started at the end of the gallery and worked his way toward the front, letting people out of their cells in groups. Once one group returned, the next would go. I noticed that the people before me were all wearing shoes on their way to the shower, so I followed suit, but when I got there I saw a majority of those same men standing under the water in their boots. "What the—? Huh? Who? Oh hell Naw! Uh-uhh." The shock of what I was witnessing was so intense I couldn't even complete my thoughts. My mind could not produce comprehensible words fast enough to keep up with my reaction. Not only was this the strangest thing that I've ever seen in my life, but it was beyond belief and it freaked me all the way out.

Like the cells, the shower too was a cage. In it were approximately fourteen or so showerheads mounted to the wall and bunched together in a tight fit. Once everyone was in, the gate was shut, locked, and dead-bolted. I was closed in there with creepy creep creeps, weirdos, and bugs (insane lunatics)— just some of everybody—and they all had on boots while they were lathering up. Please let this register. These men had their boots on so they wouldn't slip and slide on a wet floor in case all hell broke loose. People had been known to get attacked in the shower, so these men were prepared to defend themselves by any means necessary. From that moment on I wore my boots in the shower so tight my ankles throbbed.

Can you imagine having to live like that—having to prepare or be ready to defend yourself at all times? Do you understand how extremely high the stress levels are and the effects that level of stress will have on a human being mentally, emotionally, and physically year after year after year after year? These men will be released soon and be expected to merge with society and have families and other social relationships? After all the shaping, molding, influencing, and affecting that prison did to their minds, they are coming home soon, and they are bringing prison with them.

Prison is a stupid place. Regardless of how ridiculous the things are that I am explaining to you, they are real. It is an alternative world where people do things "just because," and after years and years and years of living in a heartless, vicious, and cruel world, these same people will return to the real one after having been conditioned by an extremely brutal one.

Because the time left to serve on my sentence was down to ten years, I qualified for transfer to a medium-level penitentiary and left maximum security, only to be shipped to the prison that gave me great frustration and tested my patience.

3

The Overseers

When I was a child it occurred to me
That people only see what they want to see
That people only help who they want to help
And couldn't care less about the rest
I met a blind man at the bus stop
He was from the Darfur region of Sudan
So I took his hand and gave him my seat
And said, "I'm a young man, I can stand"
He said, "I used to have sight, that's without a doubt
But what I witnessed in my country made me cry my eyes out
I came to this nation to seek out some aid
Because our men are being slaughtered and our women are
being raped
And we don't even know why
 Governments don't just displace people like this
Without there being any method to the madness
500,000 homeless and living in fear.
Many of the men are dead, and if there's fighting
It will have to be done by the women
But how can they when they are as vulnerable as the children
So I searched this nation's projects and ghetto borders

For the return of our kidnapped warriors

And the lost tribes of their ancestors, who were displaced

400 years ago by a similar fate

Who now stand strong and proud but seem a bit distracted—

And that's okay

They had a lot on their plate

As long as they understand man was born to be free

And understand that freedom costs lives

And understand that in order to be free

We would rather die on our feet than live on our knees!

—Yamini

The moment I got on the bus on my way to medium security, I was given a sign as to what was to come, and it began with the bus driver. This relic was a white, middle-aged, ignorant, overweight, out-of-shape, tobacco-spitting, repulsive loudmouth who made no attempt to mask his racism. With him were three other middle-aged, sluggish, sloppy, life-abused in the eighteenth century, raggedy looking folks who had the audacity to look at us with disgust. Their lieutenant chain-smoked like a man I knew in maximum security who had given up on life and was waiting to die. They looked so bad they made me feel good about myself, and I was the prisoner. I sat in my seat smiling and shaking my head. This was movie stuff. It couldn't be real. This can't be happening to me. Fifteen physically fit African American men were in chains transferring to another prison, and yet we were subjected to the nasty, racist attitudes of four hobos whom each of us would have had no problem crushing with our bare hands. Knowing the true reality of a no-win situation, I did what I've done since my county jail segregation incident. I kept my mouth shut and acted like those clowns didn't exist. However, these types of people were getting harder and harder for me to ignore, and unknowingly my calm demeanor was about to be pushed to the brink.

When I arrived to Western Illinois Correctional Center it was nothing like the maximum-security design. The buildings were two-story structures that looked like lowercase t's or x's in the alphabet. In fact they were called X houses for that reason. In the prison there were four of these cell houses, and surrounding them were 10-foot barbed-wire fences that traveled completely around the compound. On the grounds were several gun towers, one of which was in the center of the prison. The chow hall, multipurpose building, and administration building strategically surrounded it so that in the event of disorderly behavior in these areas, shots could be fired at targets easily.

We pulled up in front of the personal property building and the raggediest of the raggedy guards, who had a mouth full of rotten teeth, said, "All y'all just go in there. Hurry up! Move. Go in there." That's how he said it. "Y'all go in there." No care for his work and nothing professional about what he was doing. Walking into the building hoping to get the property check over and done with, I sat down in the hall outside a room that the guards used to make sure contraband wasn't being brought into the penitentiary. Then I remembered I had to go through another damn strip search. Because these guards had shown themselves to be ignorant fools, I was anticipating a serious problem in this strip search.

While sitting and waiting for my name to be called, I heard loud talking coming from the room. An argument had already started between the man who went in before me and the officer shaking down his property. From where I sat, I could hear him asking the guard if he would not mistreat his belongings and to stop throwing his things around. I said to myself, "Here we go. Here we go!" I knew it was coming. I could tell by the foul attitudes of these officers that they were going to be in that shakedown room clowning. It was so common I came to expect it.

The argument that I heard the man in front of me having was about his radio. He had an older black radio that was considered a luxury item among prisoners. Anybody with one had something special, and the guards knew how rare and important they were to the owner. Using a tone that told the prisoner he was powerless against his decision, the officer told the inmate that his radio was altered. He said the play button was stuck, and for that reason my man had to send it home or destroy it. Before the situation got completely out of hand, my traveling companion asked to see a lieutenant to oversee the issue with the hope that someone with authority would use better discretion, better reasoning—pretty much anyone not having a hateful, vindictive attitude. That was his hope. When the lieutenant walked in he was just as raggedy and scruffy looking as everybody else. He asked the officer what the problem was, and the officer said two words: "altered radio." The lieutenant replied, "Whatcha gon' do; send it home or trash it." That was it. He didn't hear an argument from the guy, nor did he care to look at the property to see if the officer was just being spiteful about the whole thing. Nothing. So the man exploded. He went completely off. He started cussing everybody in the room out and demanded that they ship him immediately.

This too was a common occurrence. When men transferred into a penitentiary and got a whiff of the mistreatment that they believed was going on or were mistreated in personal property, they would demand to be transferred. They would make threats to staff, which would get them shipped because those types of intimidating methods were reasons for immediate transfer to higher-security penitentiaries.

People were known to bug up and snap like that because, for many of them, those small personal items were the only things in this world they owned. For men who have served long prison sentences, the only thing they possess in this life are the things in those two small boxes that they carry anytime they move. No one had money. Guys were broke, starving, and gangbanging, and they didn't have family members to take care of them or help them purchase appliances that were expensive. So whenever officers would take certain things of value from prisoners that were no longer sold anywhere in the state, some men would lose it.

After the man's explosion, he was dragged out of the room, thrown in a segregation cell, and told he wasn't going nowhere and that he'd better get used to it, because they did things differently here. I was next in line and had been paying very close attention to how this operation was being run, so I was already prepared for some garbage. The officer rummaged through my property with complete disregard for my belongings. He made a pile of things that I could take into the prison with me and a pile of things that I would have to throw away or send home. I was heated. I was just as frustrated as the man before me, but I had a practice of controlling my emotions. I practiced that from the county jail years because these people here will make you want to hurt them, and they did things intentionally to tick us off.

We were in a part of the state far away from the North that was out in the boondocks. These prison employees were also farmers and former coal miners. Coming from Chicago, I wasn't used to this type of in-your-face, foaming-at-the-mouth, blunt racism. I was used to the quiet racism, the back-door smiling-in-your-face type of stuff. This was Southern. This was some Southern crap.

But like everything else, I dealt with it. I dealt with it because even though the officers were who they were, I knew how to avoid them. Not only guards but prisoners too. Some inmates are the types of men whom these harsh conditions and treatments have made so bitter that they are angry at the world and love to start all kinds of nonsense. I knew how to avoid that. I knew how to deflect conversations that could lead to arguments, and I had practice doing it. I read people's body language, which helped me to identify when something dangerous was about to go down, and I made it my business to be someplace else.

This practice was essential not only for survival but for peace of mind as well. My approach with guards and their racist attitudes and behaviors was no different. They had no reason to treat us like that. It was as if they had an opportunity to mistreat black men and they seized it. That's how I saw it. My thinking was, "They are out here by themselves, among their people, with no other ethnic groups in the area who have ever done anything to them or given them a reason to dislike them." It was as if this was an opportunity to mistreat African Americans because they didn't get a chance to in the fifties and sixties, or any time before that, and so here they were now, a prison town, filled with black and brown men, and they were chasing what they missed out on all those years.

Bringing my attention back to what was going on in the room, I squatted down over the property that I was being allowed to keep and stared at the pile I had to get rid of. In it were pictures from my family and friends that weren't in the best condition, but they were sentimental things I wanted to keep. I was being forced to get rid of them all, and it hurt. I looked over at the lieutenant, who was still in the room, and he said, "Get a bag." I knew no help was coming from him. He asked, "Whatcha gon' do; throw it away or send it home?"

I always sent my belongings home. For personal satisfaction, any property that had been confiscated, even though I had to pay for shipping and postage, I sent home. That's how the guards treated us. They wanted us to throw away our own personal property, and if we didn't, we had to pay out of our pocket; us, men with nothing; men who make 30 cents an hour. Here I was with my only possessions in this world, things that are dear to me, with two people who didn't give a damn standing over me with their faces frowned up. I thought, "These people are really trying their best to make us hate them." There was no reason or rationale that I could think of other than they wanted us angry at them. That they want it to look like all men in prison are deadly and dangerous and that their jobs are of the greatest importance because they have to handle all of these dangerous people. I had to let it go because I was heating up. I gathered what I was allowed to keep, packed it away, and left the area to go be strip-searched. Walking into the room I was anticipating more bigoted behavior, some serious vulgarities, and possibly a fight. As it turned out, the guards did not want to be in the room any longer than we did, so they quickly made us go through the proper procedures.

After the strip search I was escorted to the clothing room, where I had to get the blue shirt and pants that were standard issue statewide. The blues. I had 'em all right. The entire prison population walked around blue. I thought it was a sick joke.

There was a time before my prison sentence when the penitentiaries were wide open, meaning that the prisoners ran the prisons. Men wore jeans and other designer clothing and had cash, drugs, jewelry, large stereos, and many other material items, just like they were still in the streets. Now everyone has the same property, or has the ability to have the same property.

There is no more class system, and those prisoners who may have a financial advantage are equal with those who don't. We all dressed the same and had the same material possessions.

As soon as I set foot in the clothing area, a short 4-foot-6, loudmouthed, middle-aged white woman wearing glasses with lens so thick they looked like glass ashtrays, came bursting into the room from the back door giving instructions. "Gentlemen, the clothes that you will be issued will fit and nothing, absolutely nothing, will be loose and HANGING OFF YOUR BUTTS," she shouted.

Prison employees, regardless of whether they were administrators, health care workers, officers, or maintenance workers, hated to see young men sagging pants off their butts. She explained to us how we were not going to be allowed to sag under any circumstances and that if she saw it she was going to make sure that we got pants that fit two sizes smaller. Before she could finish addressing us in her nasty, condescending tone, two young guys walked past the building with their pants sagging. She ran out of there and chased them down like they were stealing her car. "YOUUUUU," she screamed. She called out for an officer to grab them and escort them into the clothing room. "Is everybody down here nuts?" I asked the guys who had just transferred in with me.

When she came back into the clothing room, she had the two guys she chased down with her. She said to them, "Obviously, since we can see your butts, your pants are too big, so let me get them right now please." In exchange, she gave those young men pants that were so tight they looked like leggings. "Oh, hell naw," I said in a low voice that only a few people standing nearby heard. It would have been one thing to get the guys something that fit so their pants couldn't sag, but it was something else to go to this extreme. I watched and waited to see how they were going to respond to her humiliation. They huffed and they puffed and they pouted, but in the end they accepted the embarrassment.

Whenever I saw mistreatment of any kind to prisoners who lacked the know-how or the courage to respond appropriately to the staff, I would offer sound, healthy advice. Because I had no intention of fighting another man's battle, most of the advice I gave was to "ask to speak with a white shirt," as these two young men did. When the white shirt, a lieutenant, arrived, he looked at them, shrugged his shoulders, and told them, "Either the pants or a trip to segregation; pick and choose." Each of them chose the pants and walked out of the building, across the prison grounds, and into the cell house wearing pants that hugged their thighs and butt cheeks.

Miss Lady got her point across and I understood clearly that she was someone not to fool with. What was different about her from other non-officer prison employees was the authority she had and walked around the penitentiary with. I learned that she was one of the union representatives for the officers and other workers in this penitentiary. Even though she was a civilian, the guards obeyed her orders and she did what she wanted to do.

"The clothing-room lady," as she was called by everyone, was very aggravating and annoying, but she was nowhere near the worst employee in this prison. There was an officer who was known to plant razors in the cells of people he didn't like. He and a few of his coworkers would claim to have found a razor hidden in soap or shoes or tucked away in old letters during shakedowns. What made planting razors effective for these guards was that it was hard to defend against, because it was a common weapon that was often found. Possession of one could mean six months or more of segregation and a transfer to maximum security. It was their word against yours.

I was very conscious that in these small prison towns, the employees are all from the same area. I saw these penitentiaries as family businesses, and it would be delusional for anyone to think that he was going to come into one of these small towns where everyone was raised together since childhood and get them to take his side in a matter. That is foolish, ridiculous thinking.

Watching the behaviors of the people involved in the penal institution was interesting, and I watched them all. Not just inmates but also the staff and the administration. When state administrators such as deputy directors would visit the prisons, they behaved like important delegates visiting a nation that needed their aid to exist. When they arrived, the officers and staff were always busy, busy, busy, and gave them security escorts everywhere they went. They were the superiors who ruled over their workers, who in turn had authority over the inmates. It was a world within a world. We were a "society of captives", and the people who ran this prison, who had power over us, were straight out of a novel. They were stranger than fiction imagined out of someone's creative thinking.

Without further incident I gathered my clothes and walked out of the clothing room with another inmate who was working there, and we went onto the walk (the sidewalks inside the penitentiary grounds). The moment I turned the corner, I saw a movement line with about one hundred or so prisoners leaving from one of the cell houses. The men were in pairs, walking side by side. This is how prisoners had to move every time they stepped outside the cell house. The purpose was so that the officers could keep order and an easy count of everyone who left the housing unit. Many times these lines were run by guards with nasty attitudes, and if someone were to fall behind the person they were standing next to, the officer would get irate, very mouthy, and often make derogatory comments.

The guard moving the line that I was watching was furious about something, and he got in the face of a young man who didn't look like he had much fight in him. He was pulled aside and ordered to stand right in the spot where he was while the rest of the line went into the chow hall. Normally, when an officer pulls someone out of the line, he is sent back to the cell house and misses that meal, but this young man was just standing there alone, in prison, with no one and nothing around except a gun tower 50 feet away. It was a way to insult him publicly and let everyone see that "this guy here is obedient and better not move until told."

Prison forever tests and tries people openly to see what kind of person each prisoner is. In the case of the young guy, it let everyone know, officers and the inmate population, that he was going to do what he was told when he was told, regardless of how ridiculous, demeaning, and insulting it may be. I asked the man who was helping me move my property into the cell house, "Is this how they get down in this joint?"

He said, "It's like this every single day. This place is a circus, and they have way more clowns than they need."

Walking into the cell house, I noticed something completely different than what I'd seen before. The wings were monitored by a hub that sat in the middle of the building and had officers stationed there. From that vantage point, they could see all four wings. The unit design was not bars, like in maximum security, but cell doors, like the county jail. Unlike the jail, I was given the key to my own door to let myself in and out whenever it wasn't dead-bolted.

In the front of the wing was a staircase that led up to a second level, where the row of cell doors continued. I took my key, unlocked the door, and walked into a cell that was roughly 12' x 9'. Although there was no one inside when I entered, there was a television and other personal items, which let me know I had a cellmate. Right away I was uncomfortable.

Throughout my entire fifteen years of incarceration, I had over 150 different cellmates, and anytime I moved to a different cell and my new celly wasn't in at the time, it made me uncomfortable because I didn't like when it happened to me. Walking in on a stranger convicted of God knows what and sitting in a room with everything I owned was another one of prison's realities that I never adjusted to. The invasion of privacy was intense.

Whenever a bed space in a shared cell becomes empty and the remaining person leaves the cell house for any reason during the day, chances are there will be someone new there when he returns. Sometimes he's cool, which was always my hope, but sometimes he's the unclean type who refuses to take showers, or a psychotic bug waiting on you to disrupt whatever peace you found.

I once had a cellmate go to segregation, which left my cell occupied by only me. I had been gone all morning, and when I came back, my new celly, whom I hadn't met yet, had a homemade sign sticking halfway out the door signifying that he was taking a dump. That's how we met. When he was done I tried to give the cell a little while to air out, but it was already lockup time and the officer was coming on the wing to make sure everyone had gone into their cells. The stench was stomach-turning, make-you-want-to-fight bad, so I stood near the screened hole in the door that helped to ventilate the cell with fresh air. When the odor finally dissolved, I had to fight having an attitude with a man I knew nothing of. It was unfair to him and I knew it.

After experiencing prison housing for a few years, I understood that those first encounters with new cellmates set the stage for either peaceful relationships or aggravating ones, in which the two men are constantly provoking each other. I didn't want to be trapped in a cage with someone who despised me, and I him.

There was once an ugly situation between two cellmates who hit it off bad from the jump. Both BB and Paco had opposing personalities and character traits, like on those reality shows where people have to live together, making a clash inevitable. BB had everything he needed to serve his prison bid: TV, radio, hotpot, beard trimmers, and plenty of groceries. He was well provided for; however, he was one of the stingiest people I've ever known. His cellmate, Paco, had nothing.

The two of them had been getting into it with each other real heavy about the smallest things. Paco didn't like how BB would never help him out when he was hungry or let him watch his TV when he wasn't in the cell. One afternoon, when BB was out of the building, Paco poured water into all of his electronics, destroying everything, and walked himself to segregation. The term "walking yourself to segregation" means that a person intentionally violates a rule or policy, resulting in his immediate removal from the cell house by way of handcuffs to segregation. Destroying a cellmate's property and then go run and hide in segregation was cowardly, but it was very common, and it happened all the time.

Living with people can be very trying, especially when they have disgusting habits. One cellmate of mine was a repulsive tobacco spitter, and I hated it. I couldn't stomach finding dried-up spit stains whenever he missed the toilet and was too lazy to clean it up.

Then there was one with room-clearing gas. Buffalo was a big, gentle, easy-going, 320-pound celly of mine who had a health condition that, because of the medication he was taking, caused his gas to be toxic and made being around him unbearable. There were nights when his gas was so bad it would wake me out my sleep.

But of all the problem cellmates I lived with, the greatest difficulty I had was when I knew the person moving into my cell had a reputation for despicable and vulgar behavior. I already knew what type of man he was and I hated to live with that kind of person. I did my best to conceal my dislike and treated those cellmates like human beings, but I didn't like them. There was no phony relationship where I was smiling and enjoying a good conversation. I just lived with the person and had the most basic human decency for him. If he was hungry, I would feed him. If he didn't have a TV or radio, I would let him use mine. But I didn't like him.

It is a strange balance that has to be had with a cellmate, because regardless of his crimes, this person is living in the cell with you, and this is the person you have to deal with. Cellmates have direct access to all of your personal, intimate property, which you can only protect if you are in the cell. The moment you walk out, anything can happen. Thankfully, the guy I moved in with was smooth and we had no issues.

A few weeks passed before I got my first assignment in the gym. I was surprised because it was something that was sought out by many people. What made it attractive was that it gave me an opportunity to exercise a couple of hours a day, plus it was the place where leisure-time activities for the prison were planned.

Prison assignments are just that—assignments—and there are a couple of reasons men even accept them. The first is that men with absolutely no help from the outside world do what they must to survive. Second, people need something to do instead of sit in their cells or on the wing all day. There is no real money involved, and the wages are as dehumanizing as in third world countries. As of 2011, the majority of prison jobs pay only 30 dollars a month. That equals 1 dollar a day and approximately 16 cents per hour for a six hour shift.

Working in the gym was good. It made the days go by faster, and I was eating and exercising more. On the surface, the LTS [leisure time activities] employees seemed to be fair people compared to this other bunch. Seemed! Not only did the supervisor and his staff run this department, but a few of them also sat on the board that heard inmate grievances and disciplinary reports.

Disciplinary reports are also called "tickets" and are written by all staff whenever an inmate behaves in any way that goes against the prisons policies. It is ruled by a board of two to three people, with one person usually being a civilian who also works in the prison. Punishment of an offense results in a prisoner receiving segregation time or loss of grade.

Because so many men hated C grade and didn't want to lose what little they had, a docile society was created. It made men so concerned about themselves that a sizeable portion of them became sheepish to prison administration, guards, and staff. These inmates became so afraid of losing those privileges that they began to allow their jailers to humiliate and verbally mistreat them. That was sad to see. Watching men trade in their dignity for a bag of chips, for a phone call, or so they may go outside and play bothered me to the core. But the absolute worse situation that arose from this mild form of punishment was when men became informants for no other reason than the threat of losing a few pleasures. I avoided C grade as best I could while keeping my integrity and dignity intact.

The grievance is a separate issue and maybe the most important process in a prisoner's life. It is the best avenue available for an inmate to report his mistreatment by anyone working in IDOC. Any complaint must be written, documented, and sent through the proper chain of command. Even if an action requested is denied on the penitentiary level, it can be appealed and sent to a higher state authority for further review. This is very important to prisoners.

One day I was mopping the floor outside the office and a scruffy little guard wearing clothes so big they were falling off came in and asked the LTS employee where the grievances were kept. She nodded toward the cabinet in the corner of the room, and the officer went over to it and thumbed through the files until he found what he was looking for. Looking over it thoroughly, he pulled out a grievance a prisoner had written against him and left.

A few weeks before this incident, I had written a grievance about my property being seized by an officer who claimed it was contraband. I never heard anything about it, and now I knew why. What I was told in letter from the grievance officer was that my grievance was reviewed, the claim had no merit, and it was therefore denied. This was the response that prisoners always got. Before I saw the officer going through the files, I could only speculate as to what was going on with our grievances and why none of us were receiving any remedies for our complaints.

The next morning, Short Top, a guy I worked with, and I were discussing how we were going to divide our work for the day. Jokingly, he suggested that I do way more than my share, and I responded, "Yeah, all right. I ain't doing all that." The LTS supervisor was in the office and heard me say what I wasn't doing, came out of the room, and fired me on the spot. I dropped the broom, dirty mop water, and everything else I had and headed toward the exit. He walked me back to the cell house himself and made sure the officers locked me in my cell. There was no need for me to write a grievance at that point, because I knew what was going to happen. So I wrote the warden instead. His response was, "He was going to look into it." Yeah, right.

The biggest contribution to officer mistreatment of prisoners is when prison administrators refuse to hold the guards accountable for their behavior. It created the initiative in some officers to make up rules as they saw fit. There was an instance when an officer decided that he didn't want any talking on the walk. His rule suggested that two people, two grown men, walking side by side could not continue their conversation when they stepped outside of the building. This was not a policy. It was not something that we were required to do as part of the rules and regulations of this or any other prison. As expected, it was half ignored and half obeyed.

When the made-up rule began, officers were writing tickets whenever prisoners were talking outside of the cell house, but those tickets were being thrown out by the adjustment committee. Although they lacked credibility, the officers continued their attempts to enforce a rule that did not exist. However, they changed their tactic.

Two young men were walking and talking when an officer approached them. He told them to shut up on the walk. They ignored him and continued walking, not because the rule was bogus but because of the officer's provocative behavior. Because he was ignored as if he had no authority, the guard filled with rage and, within seconds, his face looked like a reddish-purple turnip. He stomped after them, demanded their IDs, and wrote them both tickets. When they returned to the cell house, a lieutenant was radioed and the two men were handcuffed and taken to segregation. A month later I ran into one of the young guys who got caught up in that silliness, and he told me what happened. He said the officer's ticket did not claim that they had ignored the officer because they were talking but that the officer had given them a direct order that they had refused, and that the two of them had then begun cursing him out.

Ignoring the guards in this penitentiary became a common practice for me. Many of them had racist attitudes and didn't care to hide it. Whenever I ignored one of them for speaking to me with a demeaning tone, he would get extremely angry, like it was me who had humiliated him—like he was insulted that I had the audacity to disobey him. What was even worse was that such guards expected me to stand there and accept their verbal abuse until they were done. I had to walk away from these men because they would aggressively get in people's faces. It was a must that they be ignored, because the alternative had consequences that were too much for me to accept. If I didn't know about nothing else, I knew the best way to avoid an assault on an officer with belligerent behavior was to walk away.

I had an incident where it took all I had not to put my hands around the neck of one of these racist clowns. One afternoon, the wing that I lived on was coming into the cell house from the chow hall, and I was in the middle of a conversation with another man. A short, 300-pound sergeant, who was the loudest of the loudmouths, got up from his seat and in my face, screaming at the top of his lungs: "WHY ARE YOU TALKING? DO YOU UNDERSTAND THAT THERE IS NO TALKING ON THE WALK?"

I looked at the man and said, "I hear you."

He shouted back, "MY DOG CAN HEAR ME. D-O Y-O-U U-N-D-E-R-S-T-A-N-D M-E, I-N-M-A-T-E?" He was fuming and slobbering and breathing hard.

Not knowing how else to respond, I laughed in his face. I had to. He had got under my skin so deep that I was inches, and I mean inches, from a full-scale assault on this overweight, racist, middle-aged man. Laughing was the only thing I could do, and me laughing it off and walking onto the unit saved me from assaulting a correctional officer, two years of segregation, and a new case. Lord knows I wanted to get him. Oh, I wanted to get him. This sergeant made it his business to aggravate, intimidate, and frustrate every African American man he came into contact with. I was so frustrated by what just happened that I went to my cell and lay on my bunk to calm down. I did not like being in that mood. The window in the cell was open, and I could still hear him talking crazy to other people as they entered the building. The day was warm, but because I did not want to hear his voice a moment longer, I got up and closed the window.

If you were watching a prison movie and a riot kicked off and this sergeant I just described got a serious beat down, the movie watchers would cheer. That's who he was. I cannot describe his character any better way. He was the man in the movie who when he got what he had coming, the crowd roared.

When I first arrived at this medium-security prison, I was told that the facility had way more clowns working there than they needed. The officer who manned the gun tower was another one of them. I didn't know if he was a drunk or what his problem was, but he sure had the behavior of a person who is drunk on the job. What I did know, though, was that he was dangerous. Whenever prisoners came out of the cell house onto the walk, he would slide open the window to the gun tower so hard the sound echoed. Then he would lean the entire top half of his body out of the window, swaying back and forth like a wino, all while swinging his assault gun and screaming at the men in the line below to keep it deuced up (in pairs of two).

I wish there were surveillance cameras somewhere that could confirm what I'm telling you. I really wish you could see this fool hanging out that tower window swinging his gun and talking crazy. I was always nervous around him because I had never seen that kind of reckless behavior from a prison guard with an assault weapon. I would say to myself, "God Almighty, please don't let him shoot nobody. Lord, get me out of this place. They just don't care."

Even the chaplain, the person responsible for the religious services and for making sure that prisoners of different faiths were able to congregate on their holy days, was stone cold out of his mind. He was as ignorant as they come, and I had no idea how he came to have that position of leadership. Not only did he interefere with the faith anyone who wasn't Christian, he also had a strong dislike for anyone who was not of the denomination that he was.

Proving to the inmate population how much he didn't give a damn, the chaplain once allowed the disinformation on a religion to be passed out by the members of his denomination. In the same manner that small, uneducated religious groups do when they want to demonize or halt the progression of another faith, misinformation was spread through pamphlets.

One morning I was walking through the dayroom and I saw a small stack of pamphlets placed neatly on a bench. I picked one of them up, as I normally do whenever I see books or reading materials sitting on a table for anyone to come by and take. The pamphlets said that all Muslims are idol worshipers, that every morning they get up and pray to the God of the Sun when it rises, and that the practice is similar to the practice of the ancient Aztec civilizations. I gathered all the pamphlets, threw them in the garbage, and asked all my friends who lived on other wings if they saw them to throw them in the garbage too. I never confronted the chaplain about it because there was no need. I just kept throwing the trash that he allowed to be passed out about different religions in the garbage. That's what we were dealing with in this prison. These people working here were nuts, and the administration did nothing to stop their malicious behavior and attitudes toward us.

Although Western Illinois had a depressing and dreary atmosphere, at least it had an outstanding four-year college operating out of it. As provoking a place as the prison was, I was very determined not to allow it to affect me in any way. The moment schooling became available, I signed up to take courses that allowed me to pursue an associate's degree. To get in school

I had to submit my name to the school coordinator, who then put me on a waiting list. Sometimes the wait time was so long that it made people lose interest and ask for assignments to help them pass time. In my case, three months had passed before I received a letter in the mail saying I had been accepted and telling me where to report when the next module began.

My first class was psychology, and not only was I taking a needed requirement for the degree, I was also learning about human thought process and the factors that influence environmental conditions and behaviors. Sitting in those classes listening to men who hadn't seen the world in ten, fifteen, or twenty years debate about the state of the world's affairs was borderline stupid, but funny as hell.

Going to school made it easy for me to stay away from foolishness, but that didn't mean foolishness was going to stay away from me. This was prison after all. A person will be tested. One day, a cellmate of mine went home, making my cell open for a new person to move in. As I stated earlier, new cellmates can sometimes disrupt your peace. This time, which I believe was out of spite from the cell-house sergeant, my new celly was one of the prostitutes involved in some of the sexual misconduct that was going on. At no time in my sentence had I ever lived with one of these men. They will use your small cage, living space for two people, for their sexual acts. They have no other place to do it.

The day the prostitute moved into my cell, I knew I was targeted. In response I gathered all of my belongings, packed up, and refused housing. Refusing housing is a method that prisoners use when they don't want to live in a particular cell or cell house. I knew better than to tell a person that he cannot move into a cell. Any time a person tells another person that he cannot move into a cell, he will be written a ticket for intimidation or threats, which could get him anywhere from three to six months of segregation. I knew not to do that; especially when I believed he was purposely sent. I wasn't about to fall for the okie-doke setup and be charged with interfering in administrative decisions. I had more sense than that.

For refusing housing, I was given ten days of segregation because the offense wasn't serious and no officer or inmate was harmed, intimidated, or threatened. This was the first time I had ever been to seg in the Illinois Department of Corrections. I had been before in the Cook County Jail, so I pretty much expected the same situation. Thankfully, this time there were no memorable moments. It was quick, easy, and needed. I needed that privacy; I needed those ten days alone to be with my thoughts and not to have to look at, smell, or talk to another stranger whose issues could burden a mountain. I had me to deal with, and surviving in a mentally and emotionally hostile prison environment was more than enough. I took what we called a little vacation, and it turned out to be a peaceful ten days. God is greater, and He has a way of making something good come out of what we may think is bad.

When I got out of seg, I immediately wrote a letter to the school administrators so that I could get back on the list, and I was told that it would be a few months. The waiting list to get back academic courses was longer than I could bear, so I took a computer class instead. Because I had no computer literacy and the world was moving ahead at light speed, I didn't want to reenter society like somebody who just arrived from another planet. I had no real knowledge of how the world was moving except what I saw on TV and what my family kept me informed about.

When the class began, the teacher was very apologetic for us using software that was completely outdated, as if any of us knew the difference. For me, it was something different from the reading and writing that I had done forever, and it consumed six hours of my day. I completed my typing, Word, and Excel books and was beginning to comprehend computer language. The course was going well, and as much as I appreciated it, it didn't last long. The penitentiary atmosphere is volatile and unpredictable, and anything that can happen, will happen.

One evening, after two months had passed in my computer course, a few guys who had been in school all day were exercising outside of their cells. They weren't able get to the yard or gym regularly with the rest of the wing, and so to compensate for missing valuable workout time, a group of us got together and exercised in the dayroom. Working that evening was one of those ornery officers who loved to show his authority; he told the guys they weren't supposed to be working out in the dayroom. He was not our normally assigned wing officer and he had a bad attitude, telling everyone who was exercising that they would be receiving tickets.

Most nights I would have been getting it in with the group, but that night I was watching the NBA draft and Yao Ming just went number 1. After the officer collected all of their IDs, he told the inmates to come to the front of the wing to see the sergeant. Upset that the guard was picking on my guys, I walked to the front, gave my ID to the officer, and told him I was working out too. When I did this, five other people did the same, supporting the men because we all exercised out there and we never had a problem. Recognizing an act of prisoner solidarity, the officer in the hub called for backup as more and more inmates approached the door to the wing entrance. The numbers were increasing fast, and people were just flinging their IDs into the hall.

Any time solidarity or unity was shown by a group of prisoners, the administration moved in to eliminate it quickly. Because the charge of inciting a riot carries a one-year segregation term, it is the greatest reason why so many people stay away from anything that resembles a union. It is also the hardest ticket to beat.

When men began coming forward and tossing their IDs out in the hall, one of the more racist lieutenants was radioed. Once he arrived, he didn't ask any questions about what was going on and called in for a support team to lock down the wing. For volunteering to go down with the ship, I was handcuffed and paraded off to segregation along with the original six men who were working out.

It was the month of July, the middle of summer, and it was H-O-T. Seg was the last place I wanted to be in those dangerous temperatures. My cell was so hot the walls were sweating, paint was peeling, the floors were toasty warm, and the heat radiating through the steel beams on the bunk bed warmed the mattress. Most prisons around the state allow fans in segregation, because the cells can become ovens. The seven of us were put in those cells under extreme conditions at a time when fans were not allowed. Although this was clearly a health issue, the guards spitefully upheld the policy that said no appliances were permissible.

Trying to do whatever we could to get cool, we asked for cups of ice that were supposed to be passed out whenever the heat rose to excessive temperatures. The officers ignored our requests, even though prisoners in segregation and population were supposed to be receiving ice or cold water several times per shift. I refused to accept not being heard, so I called all the men together to come to their doors and we devised a way to get the attention of the guards. The plan was that every ten minutes someone different would bang on the door, ask for a nurse, and say he couldn't breathe or that the heat was killing him. A request to see a nurse was almost always granted, because in the penitentiary, men had many different types of health issues— gunshot wounds, stab wounds, bad hearts, HIV treatments, all kinds of stuff. After a while the first-shift officers and nurses were so angry and annoyed that they didn't respond anymore. They told us that if we didn't stop making noise, banging on doors, and calling for the nurse that they'd make sure every shift knew not to give us anything.

I don't know how high the temperature was back there in that sweat box, but my skin was irritated. An entire shift passed, and nothing. The officers refused to even come on the wing, so our tactic had to be changed. Once again I called my buddies and suggested we take turns lying on the floor like we had passed out. We were all in agreement, and it wasn't but five minutes later that an officer came on the wing making rounds. In the very first cell he looked, he saw my buddy Preacher Man lying out on the ground like he was dying.

In the beginning of the protest it was only the seven of us who went to segregation together who were involved in our strategies for decency, but after a few failed attempts and still a strong resolve, that seven of us influenced the entire seg population to participate. All we wanted were our fans so that we could lie under them and keep cool. We didn't want ice. We didn't want water. We wanted to be cool twenty-four hours, around the clock, without having to wait to be distributed ice whenever the guards so felt.

When the officer saw Preacher Man lying down on the floor, he immediately called for the nurse, and when she arrived he told her that he was having trouble breathing. She made a call on her radio for someone to take him to the health-care unit, and then she began looking in other cells. She saw men on the floors with their mattresses, and others leaned up against walls. After seeing a bunch of men looking weak and dehydrated, the nurse immediately called for help, went cell to cell doing well-being checks, and brought everyone big cups of ice.

As the nurses went around the seg unit, they were followed by two smug-looking officers scooping and pushing what looked like a big laundry basket filled with ice. When they got to my door, the guard who had the scooper peeked in my cell and said, "None for you. I know you started this!" Wearing an expression of pleasure on his face to show how pleased he was to punish me, I was surprised by how much I wasn't even bothered. I didn't trust the ice no way. These two officers seemed too willing to pass it out after the strong resistance to it. "I bet these two dirty dogs did something to that ice," I thought. Their characters were vile enough for it to be probable, and mama didn't raise no fool.

Even though my skin was warm, I learned how to stay cool. The summers in maximum security were always hot. I would run my head and feet under water, or keep my feet in water in the sink. I also would rinse my face, arms, and legs every ten minutes or so. My enjoyment was seeing the plan work, seeing everybody else get ice and get cooled down. I was just glad that we were able to out-think them.

The next morning an officer came to my cell and told me I was moving away from the other men to an isolated part of segregation. There were only a handful of men back there in those cells, and I had no idea this part of segregation was even there. Because these other surveillance cells were stationed near the officers' work area, there was a large industrial fan blowing to keep them cool while they worked. The strong breeze drifted down the narrow corridor, creating a small wind tunnel. The hallway was silent, the corridor was cooler, and the new cell was large. It had to be 15 feet long and 15 feet wide, which was a luxury in prison. It was perfect. I said to myself, "Thank you, Lord!" Knowingly or unknowingly, the guards did me a favor and put me in a better situation than I had ever been in around the front, where it was hottest. They were punishing me with isolation, but it turned out that I received the biggest reward. Again, God is greater than anything I can imagine.

For a few weeks I sat alone, exercising, reading, and enjoying a space that was like a nice-sized bedroom, when I received a piece of mail about the board's decision on the ticket I was written. I was prepared for the worst, because I knew the kind of people I was dealing with. I knew they wanted to make examples out us for what had happened back in the cell house and in seg. As expected, the disciplinary board recommended a harsh penalty to the warden. They suggested that I get one year of segregation, one-year loss of visits, one-year loss of phone privileges, one-year C grade, and a transfer to maximum security. This is called "a year across the board." It means that every privilege that I had, the board suggested that I lose them all for a year. But again, I was shown mercy. The warden rejected the board's recommendation and instead gave me two months' loss of everything and an immediate transfer to a different medium-security facility. That was a victory to me.

Yes, I got two months' loss of privileges and a transfer, but a transfer out of that southern plantation was nothing but a victory. Also, my friends and I received very little retribution from the administration. There were no serious casualties, which is unusual whenever prisoners come together to fight for decency. Usually, there is a group of men who suffer a great deal to get basic human treatment for the rest of the population but, in our case, a few months' segregation and a transfer was the extent of the punishment.

4

Maturity

I heard what they said

But I paid them no mind

Because the content of their speech is considered unkind.

Although our skin complexions are similar

And intentions may be vain

However, just because we look alike our souls are not the same!

—Yamini

Sitting in seg those two months gave me a lot of time to think. It gave me time to reevaluate and reassess my life and any foolish decisions that I was making that put me in situations that caused more problems than I needed. I had a strong dislike for the way prisoners were being treated by guards, but at the same time I was ashamed of many of the men I was imprisoned with for behaving like savages. It was easy to become an angry black man, because in prison's barbaric culture there was so much, and so many reasons, to hate. The dismal environment alone was enough. Being away from family and friends and having my life controlled by others was e-n-o-u-g-h. For me to add more problems to what was an already burdensome, burdensome life was just stupid.

A few days after I was recommended for segregation time, I was transferred to Pinckneyville Correctional Center. Once I arrived I went straight to the prison's segregation to finish out my punishment in what is called a seg-to-seg transfer. I was tired of living like this; spiritually and emotionally exhausted from everything that I was doing wrong in my life. I had enough of foolish decision-making and foolish thinking. I couldn't take it anymore, and in that cell I prayed. I prayed and prayed and prayed like I have at no time in my life before or since. I completely submitted. I prayed, "God, please give me the life that you intend for me. Please don't let me be a stupid fool. I don't want to be a disappointment to my Creator, to my family, or to any people who may depend on me, may need me, or may call on me for help."

I was down on my knees for what seemed like hours, so long my knees hurt. When I tried to stand, a sharp pain shot through my body so fast my eyes watered. I had to rise very slowly, and when I looked, my knees were raw and bruised. I made it my business to transform my life into one that was dignified and respectful, one that appreciated people for their help. That's what I prayed for—that I get my life in order so that one day I could have a family and help get my family in order. I didn't want what this world had to offer anymore. I was done with it.

Prison changed my perception completely. I was on the inside looking out, and within those fortified walls designed to keep us away from disturbing the peace of society, I saw the misery that resulted from the good times that I and everyone around me were so harmfully influenced by. It was a lie, a trick, and I wanted to see my life properly. I didn't want to be burdened by other men and their ridiculous behaviors because of my associations with them. I wanted freedom not only from prison but from people. I was now twenty-five years old and I wanted the good life. Whenever anyone asks me when my turning point was, I tell them about that prayer of submission that day in segregation.

Early in my sentence I associated myself with people who had so many problems and issues that their messes became my messes. No longer; I'll holla. I disassociated myself from any people and any groups who didn't want a decent, dignified life. I wanted to return to the way I was raised, to the foundation that my parents fought so hard to establish for me and my brothers and sisters, who have gone on to have successful lives.

After that exhausting prayer I took a nap, and when I woke up I was walking on air. For the first time in my life I felt like a heavy burden had been lifted from me, like all the weight of the world was gone. I felt like a new man, a new human being, and as soon as my segregation time was over, the first thing I did was find people I associated myself with and told them no more. No more, no more, no more. I'm completely done with those associations—and I never felt better.

Becoming a man was so revealing it was like magic. I had a new spirit and no problems, and from that point forward not only did I carry myself with integrity, I also spoke intelligently. I immediately signed up for school to finish where I left off in the previous prison, and by God's grace I was able to get on a list and in a classroom within forty-five days. That was quick by any standard, and I approached my schooling like a man on a mission.

Trying to get an education in the penitentiary was challenging for many prisoners and for different reasons, but the most problematic for me was being housed on the school wing. Because I was taking classes full time, I had to live on a housing unit that was more revolting than any other wing I had previously been on. It was the place where many men wanted to be simply because of the privileges that were given to anyone taking classes. Living on the unit injured my soul and put me in a foul mood because there were quite a few prostitutes enrolled as well. And wherever the prostitutes went, the tricks were sure to follow.

Men who loved tricking with prostitutes signed up for school courses regardless of whether they needed them or not. They would get in the way of people who really wanted an education and put their names on the lists because they met the qualifications. However, their intent was to move to the wing to be close to the person they were having a secret affair with or to get sexual favors. Others would follow them because they were pimping, so they said. As sick and disturbing as it is, it is the truth.

Whenever prostitutes are on a wing in the cell house, the officers watch it more closely, and because this type of freaky business was going down on our wing, other prisoners in the penitentiary called it a brothel. I had to live on that nasty unit, and there was nothing I could do about it but be upset or stay in my cell. I had to deal with it and move on. I was there for my education, and this was the price I had to pay.

I had become aggravated by knowing and sometimes hearing these men during their acts. I hated that I knew what they were doing, and I hated that I had to be reminded of their sexual activities every time I walked onto the wing and there was a foul odor in the air that took my mind to their business. I was so disturbed by my environment, it almost made me crack.

I'm going to spare you any more details of what went down here because you already know. What is important to understand is that everything I explained was part of the harmful prison culture that was trying its hardest to influence me with its fashioning, molding, shaping, and developing.

A few times a year, guests were invited to come in and speak to the inmate population with positive motivational messages. Black History Month always kicked off these invitations and I was eager to know who was coming. This year, three elderly women with very long histories of doing humanitarian work around the world came to speak to us about being men. The eldest of them was well known and had been working as a chaplain inside of the penitentiaries for close to fifty years. With her were two poets and a musician.

For two hours they explained in detail how anyone of us who sat idle in prison and did not use his creative expression was exhibiting a form of death. They inspired us to write and write and write—to tell the world who we are, regardless of what we're going through. Motivated by what I heard, I immediately went back to my cell and began writing. I had so much going on inside of me that I could no longer hold it in. What came out was this:

Today I heard three queens speak
And they informed me of who I was.
Wait a minute; today I heard three queens speak
Do you know what that means, three queens speak
To souls not flesh, to spirits not bones
Understand what that means, three queens

And they informed me of who I was

And they looked like the grandmothers of my friends

So I sat and listened. . . . No, wait, I didn't listen, I paid keen attention to . . . No, that's not it either.

Forgive me for rambling but I'm trying to tell you what I felt when . . . That's it!

Today I heard three queens speak and they told me who I was

And I witnessed words break free from their mouths as if they were held captive and assumed the form of sentences.

Yeah, I witnessed words break free from their mouths as if they were held captive and assumed the form of sentences.

Then they approached me and . . . No, that's not what they did.

They . . . They . . .   Forgive me

again because I'm trippin'.

I need you to understand because you weren't there.

Where were you anyway?

I was there that day and I heard three queens speak and they told me who I was.

Oh, the words

The words that took forms of sentences had eyes and they sought me out.

They had eyes and were searching the crowd for me. The words could see and they had eyes   Then

they saw me and seized me and wrapped me like wire. . . . No,

like palm-leaf fiber and penetrated my eardrums making me
temporarily deaf.
I could no longer hear.
The words entered into my bloodstream and captured my heart.
It pumped meaning and not blood to the rest of me.
I could no longer hear, but I felt, words.
Today I heard three queens speak and they informed me of who I
was
And they looked like the grandmothers of my friends
And I heard . . . No, I felt their words!
—Yamini

This was the first poem I had ever written and I felt compelled to write it.

For peace of mind, I stayed out of the dayroom, away from the vulgarities, and was blessed to have Kareem, a good, smooth cellmate. Kareem and I jammed immediately from the first day we met. He welcomed me into the cell in the same hospitable manner that I welcomed strangers, and it put me at ease. As time went on and I grew more comfortable with him, we would have conversations about each other's families. I got to know his sons' names, and he knew the names of all five of my brothers and sisters. I didn't talk about my family to just anybody. No way. That wouldn't be smart. I did it after we were in the cell for a while and I got to know his character better.

Kareem and I also would discuss our future aspirations for ourselves and what we wanted for our families. Although he still had some involvement with his gang, it was easy for me to see that his heart wasn't in it. I was just glad to have an intelligent person I could have a sensible conversation with, share what was was going on in my head, and show pictures of my family to. That had to be guarded. Some men were so vile I wouldn't dare show them pictures of my sisters, or any other female family members, because they would slobber all over them.

I was sitting in the dayroom one evening and had my pictures spread out on the table to sort through them, and a guy I knew walked up and asked if he could check them out. I didn't mind because I understood that men loved to see pictures of free people doing free-people things, even if it was just somebody sitting on a couch. He came across a picture of one of my sisters and sat straight up like a stalking cat ready to pounce on its prey. "Aww, man, who is this? Hook me up," he said in a frantic, perverted way.

Ticked off that he was that thirsty, I used a slow, deliberate, but icy tone and said, "Ain't no way in hell I would invite you into her life." He was offended and I didn't care. I wanted him and everybody else in hearing distance to know that I, Omar

Ismail Yamini, was not going to introduce my sisters, or any woman I knew, to any of them—ever. I knew better. I knew how too many of them think. I saw them in their behaviors around the prison. I would be at fault if I were the one who introduced to a woman a person who was all in with this ugly, disgraceful environment.

I told Kareem what had happened with the pictures and he laughed and said that there was some real thirst-ball stuff going on lately. Being thirsty is when a person tries his best to get all of anything and everything he can. It doesn't matter what it is. He wants the whole meal, the leftovers, and the scraps. He has absolutely no standards and nothing to lose. Sadly, he takes this same approach with women.

Thirsty Mac was a man I knew who spent all of his time trying to slick anybody out of anything. He was one of the sorriest people I have ever come across. This fool would spend hours and hours playing on the phone, making collect calls by dialing random numbers while hoping that some curious, gullible woman would answer. If he was successful and a woman answered, he would run whatever game or scam that he concocted on her. He had absolutely no shame and even ran his game on children. After a week of predatory fishing, Thirsty Mac's persistence finally paid off in "catching a stang" (a naïve person easily tricked out of anything). A woman accepted his call, and he carried on a long conversation with her that led to further calls, which led to her visiting him and sending him money. He bled her dry and was proud of himself. Disgracefully, a couple of other men saw Thirsty Mac "come up" and they too got thirsty and started preying on women and children over the phone. Damn!

I wanted to know what else had been going on around the camp, because on this wing, I stayed in my cell a lot. I was aware of a few fights between cellmates on the unit, and one of them was an example of the madness of this world.

There were two cellmates, Dano and Ball, who had a big falling out. It came to light that Ball was reading Dano's mail whenever he was out of the cell. He came across a letter, picture, and the phone number of a woman Dano had recently met and had been writing. In a bold, bold move, Ball called his cellmate's lady friend flirting and trying to take her from him. When Dano found out, he attacked his celly, smashing two of his own appliances across Ball's head and cutting him so deep he had to go to an outside hospital.

As crazy as this may sound, men stealing phone numbers and addresses of women from their cellmates or other prisoners was not unusual. These people were so thirsty for companionship, or someone to send them anything, that they didn't care about the consequences which were always, always severe. For this reason, all prisoners guarded their mail like precious gems.

A few days after Dano's assault on Ball, I was out on the yard playing basketball when I saw Tino, a man whose family I knew from the streets, climbing up and down a barbed-wire fence that was nearby. "Look, Tino trippin' again," one of the guys on the court said. Seconds later an officer in the nearest gun tower leaned out his window and yelled at him, asking him if he wanted to get shot today. Immediately Tino jumped down off the fence and walked away looking at the ground like a scolded child. Ignoring him because we all knew he had some kind of mental issue, we got back to our game. Within minutes I heard loud laughter and cheers coming from over by the track where people did their running and jogging, and again, our game had paused. Tino was out on the track, striding in perfect form, buck naked. I fell out laughing. This was too much. Officers had to come out from their stations to get him and they weren't happy. For his ridiculous performance, Tino went to seg for a couple of weeks, but don't think he was done acting a fool.

As soon as he returned to population, Tino pulled his biggest stunt yet. No one ever knew what things set him off, and nobody cared. I always thought he did these things for attention because, talking and interacting with him, I got the sense that he understood exactly what he was doing. But something was obviously wrong with this man.

Only out of seg a couple of days, Tino was in the dayroom late one morning on the top deck with a homemade rope he created by tearing long strips from his blanket. He knotted the ends of it together for lenth and then tied one end of the rope to the top deck bannister. The other he loosely wrapped around his neck. Then he jumped. Fortunately for Tino, the rope was poorly manufactured. But because the blanket was cheap as hell it had a bungee-cord effect that yanked this fool back up just enough for the strip around his neck to come undone and tangle around his shoulder. He was just hanging there with a stupid, painful look on his face. A couple of officers rushed on the wing in disbelief but after seeing who it was slowly swinging back and forth they stared at him as if contemplating whether they were going to cut him down or leave. The drop from the second floor to the first was only about 12 to 15 feet so there was no sense of urgency.

Shortly after Tino's failed suicide attempt, Kareem suffered a great loss. His young son died in a car accident. It was a hard, tough time for him, and I felt his pain. I had learned so much about li'l man through our many conversations. Kareem and I had become friends and I enjoyed his company. He was also a good man who had been making terrible decisions that finally landed him in prison. However, he was working very hard to turn his life around. Before the tragedy I had encouraged him to quit his kitchen assignment and go to school so he could start working on that future he wanted for his sons. Kareem didn't have one of those long prison sentences and was headed home in a couple of years. He was my buddy and I grieved with him in our small, bathroom-sized living space, and for a couple of weeks, I kept a very close eye on him.

I've seen many men I considered friends cope with the loss of loved ones, and most of them took it hard for not being there for their family in their time of need; men who believed their sons and daughters and other family members died because they weren't there. To see these people feel responsible for the injuries or deaths in their families and then have to go into a cell, a cage, and have the door or bars slam shut, to be left alone to deal with the devastation, was cold and disheartening.

The phone call was also painful to see. Watching a man on the phone and observing his behavior gave me a good idea of what news just came across. That was a dreadful time. Certain counselors, when I saw them coming, I knew bad news was coming with them. It was excruciating. The only thing you can do for the man is try to feel his pain, because he's getting ready to be told that his mother or father or son or daughter died, that his sister or brother died. God, I hated prison!

A few months went by and Kareem was doing better, but he was never the same. I felt bad for him because I was in a good place. I learned to deflect what was going on around me so I could enjoy the peace I found, which had been lost since I left my family and real friends and ventured out into the streets.

There is a foolish comment that many men share throughout the penitentiary, and that is "If you scared, go to church." To me it was one of the more ridiculous repeated phrases because it suggested that any person wanting to follow his faith instead of participating in a behavior and lifestyle that led the person to prison in the first place, was scared. It also insinuated that the only reason men turned to religion was because they were afraid that someone was going to do something to them, and so they ran to be a part of faith-based groups.

Completely ignoring this sentiment of backwards thinking people, I got involved with the religious community on a level that I had not previously been. Being raised in a God-fearing family and being blessed to be taught sane religious faith provided me with a foundation that many men didn't have. Not acting like a person who knew more than other people, I shared everything I understood the best way I knew how. Appreciating what I had to share, a short time later I was called on by the men in our community to help teach our religion.

Who knew? I know I didn't. In that group were men just like myself—they had had enough of their previous associations with people who meant them no good, and they too were working to improve their lives. A 60-year-old man who was just learning how to read and write told me that his newfound faith brought him peace for the first time in his life. He said he had done so many things to so many people that the only thing that was going to save him was God's mercy and nothing else. I felt him with that. We all did. I myself had allowed some influences to pull me away from the life that my parents worked so hard to keep me from, and despite my family's encouraging influence, I still found a way to the penitentiary. I was just trying to get back to my original nature.

I enjoyed serving the religious community. I was 28 years old and had picked up good study habits. I was in such a good place in my personal life that I forgot that riffraff were everywhere, and I learned another life long lesson. On the surface, men were claiming that they wanted to clean up their lives, and in doing so they found their way to our religious group. However, they brought all kinds of, problems, egos, jealousies, and hatreds with them; you know, garbage. Some of the people were active gang members who had positions of authority in their gangs. They would come over to the religious service bringing their twisted, gangbanging mentalities with them, trying very hard to inject their polluted thinking into the group.

One afternoon, a good friend of mine, Keith, was speaking to a group of men about behavior choices. His subject matter was something a few of the gang members didn't like, even though much of what he said was pulled straight from scripture. It was straight out the book. A short, frail, little man in very poor health and a couple of his friends approached Keith because they felt he targeted them. The little man was the most offended and wanted to fight but was in no condition to do so; however, he told Keith that one of his guys standing there with him wanted to holla at him in the bathroom. I couldn't believe it. My disbelief was not because the little fella was angry about the talk but because he was about to have someone else go and fight for him, go and defend his honor. It was nuts, and I flat out was not going to stand by and allow these men with their gang mentalities to come in and bring that harmful thinking to our faith-based group. I told the men wanting trouble that I supported Keith and said, "If it came to it, then we all gon' be fighting up in here."

Taking that position against those types of men made me stronger. I had many disagreements with gang leaders but never a fight with any of them. I spoke to them in ways that were not confrontational or offensive, but every once in a while, men like those three had to be stopped. I had to learn to deal with these men because they were gang members and drug dealers and people involved in all kinds of harmful lifestyles. They had serious problems with another person not affiliated with their group giving them instruction of any kind. I had to subtly let them know that they had no authority among us and even invited the leadership among the gangs to read, with their own eyes, what scripture said about whatever issue they were having. I kept my opinions out of it. I would tell them, "It's not me you're arguing with. Your beef is with the one who revealed what you read, not me. I ain't got nothing to do with it." Some of them never came back, whereas others accepted it—but not with goodwill.

Months passed by very quickly and school was going well. I finished all of my English requirements and was actively talking to young men to see which of them wanted anything better than a life in prison. The gang members in our religious group became less and less a problem; however, the person I will call "The Brother," who was selected as leader for our group, began to have some power-trip and ego issues. He couldn't handle a simple position that didn't require much work and began to behave as if he had authority over us.

I never forgot the fact that I was a prisoner and these people with the keys to the front gate were my captors. I also never forgot that these men whom I lived with—prisoners I struggled with and went hungry with—all suffered from the same circumstance. Although some of them were people that I would have no connection or relationship with in the free world because of their twisted thinking and behavior, suffering with them under prison's harsh, extreme, and inhumane circumstances gave us a common bond.

Brother was very eager to speak to and please those in the administration. I felt something wasn't quite right with him in the beginning, but I thought he was one of those people who did just enough brownnosing and tap-dancing to keep the chaplain pleased. His too-friendly relationship with the chaplain was the sign. It was a fight with this man to keep our service in the first place, and he treated us all with a strong dislike. He made our visits to service as annoying and aggravating as he possibly could. Whenever we came to the chapel, he would have the officers shake us all down to see if anyone had contraband or was bringing anything to the building that he was not supposed to have. This was common practice, so no one cared. What wasn't common, though, was how he would sneak around picking up people's books and notebooks and thumb through them and read their content. None of us liked that at all, and his intended aggravation was beginning to work.

Weeks went by and the chaplain's malicious provoking increased. In his final act of contempt, he told our community that we could no longer call each other by the names that were attributes of God and that as long as we were in that building, we had to call each other by the names on our IDs. That stopped 75 percent of people from coming. He was too much to deal with. Brother, however, continued to be buddy-buddy with the chaplain and voluntarily gave information to this man even though he showed us all how much he disliked our religion. It was a message to us that he was not to be trusted.

Things were bad in our group, but then they got worse. Brother began to work with the head chaplain and officers from internal affairs, revealing detailed information about the men in our community and elsewhere in the prison. He would also, allegedly, have internal affairs investigate people he may have gotten into arguments with.

That is as dangerous as it gets in prison. Somehow, some way, Brother forgot who these prisoners were. He must have forgotten that these weren't the ordinary service-going people in the world who put on their nice clothes and gather their children to go to their houses of worship on their holy days. These were former killers and ex-gangbangers who were trying to get their stuff together.

People started disappearing from population. They were being snatched up and sent to segregation because Brother had turned them in, claiming that they had threatened him. On my way to service one afternoon, I ran into him and asked him about the allegations swirling around. Boldly and unapologetically Brother said, "Look man, I'm cleaning up the joint and having people removed." His statement froze me. I don't know what I was expecting him to say, but it wasn't that.

"That's not your job, and it's dangerous," I said. "You are turning men in to people who don't give a damn if we live or die."

He said, "The chaplain told me there were some people trying to undermine me, and now I see." Disturbed by his response, I didn't say another word. I was finished with this man, so I turned around and went back into the cell house.

Later that evening, as I was cleaning my cell and thinking about how things were unfolding, an officer came and told me I was wanted in the internal affairs office. I was expecting this. I so expected it that I had already packed up all of my property and gone around the cell house collecting the belongings that I had let other people borrow. I walked over to the building thinking how pathetic a drama this had all become. Inside the lieutenant's office, Brother, the person whom people had been accusing of treason, was already sitting there. Word had spread throughout the penitentiary about what was going on in our religious community, and whenever a prisoner is known to be working with prison guards and administrators against the inmate population, that word travels like lightning. I was embarrassed as hell. We were a group of men who claimed to be God-fearing people doing things the right way, but here we were on Front Street displaying the same behaviors, placed in the same category, and facing the same scrutiny as gangs, white supremacists, and any other security-threat groups.

The lieutenant didn't waste any time with his questions. He said, "Yamini, I heard you all have a problem and the two of you need to work together to fix it." The internal affairs supervisor knew how dangerous the situation had become and still was trying to use Brother, even though word had spread throughout the joint that he was an agent working for the administration.

Understanding how little concern he had about our well-being, I said to the lieutenant, "This can't be fixed. There is no more trust with this man and the rest of us. There's nothing I could do at this point. No one will pray with him or allow themselves to be led in prayer by him."

In one last attempt he said, "If you two cannot work together, then I'll have to send both of you to segregation."

Not budging an inch I said, "I'm sorry, lieu, but this problem can't be fixed, and I hate to say it but we got to go to seg. This is done. It's over and there's no need in faking like it could be fixed."

"All right," he said. "Stand up and put your hands behind your back." He then handcuffed me and walked me out the door and across the parking lot to the segregation unit. This was how I arrived in Pinckneyville, and it was how I was about to leave, in segregation, in another seg-to-seg transfer.

A few days passed and I didn't know what to expect, because the circumstances of my segregation were completely different. I knew how charges could be trumped up because of how closely Brother was working with internal affairs; however, I did not know until a couple of days had passed how close that relationship really was.

After chow one afternoon, I got a piece of mail from the prison informing me what internal affairs was charging me with. The letter said, "A confidential informant told the internal affairs officer that I told the brother that if he did not step down from being the leader of our group that I would have him forcibly removed." I looked at the paper in disbelief. Before this news, I was thinking I would be in seg for thirty days tops for telling IA I wasn't going to cooperate. Nope. I had been charged with intimidating and threating an inmate—a charge that carries three to six months across the board.

Another couple of days had passed when I received my final verdict from the adjustment committee. It was the worst-case scenario: six months across the board. Although the charge did carry that much seg time, it was usually only given when an officer or any member of the staff was threatened. For a prisoner to receive that many months for that charge, without physical contact or inmates or guards who witnessed the action, was uncommon.

Angry and frustrated, I sat in that prison within the prison wondering where I went wrong. Did I handle this whole thing the right way? I wasn't running around backbiting guys and dragging people's name through the mud. I treated everyone like I wanted to be treated and dealt with the situation as best I could under the circumstances. What was happening now was part of the fight, part of the struggle, and so I accepted whatever ruling or whatever punishment the prison administration had for me with dignity.

Unlike most segregations in medium-security prisons, Pinckneyville's was large, capable of holding people for long-term seg bids. There were a handful of other men serving six months or more, so I assumed that I would do mine there as well. When the news came that I was being transferred to Menard, the place that it all began, it was a shock. Troubled that I had to go to Menard's segregation, the last place on earth a person wants to be, I felt a little depression creeping in. I was feeling tired all the time and had no energy to do anything. The smallest thing, like someone calling my name, bothered me. For one week I was in this funk, and I hated it so much I fought it off with all my being. I read my scripture and other novels and exercised twice a day in my tiny one-man cell until I returned to my normal self. I was just glad that no one saw me like that.

One day, while I was doing push-ups, a letter slid under my door. It was addressed to me, but in the top-left corner was the name of a woman I didn't know. Her name was Carrie. I looked at it again, carefully checking the ID number to make sure that she had the right person. Yep, it was me. Curious who this woman was and what she wanted with me, I opened it, sat down, and read the letter. Through the entire reading, I could feel her spirit. It was just what I needed. The letter came to me from an unknown, unseen person, at a period in my life when I was going through the hardest time. I was really hurting with this new segregation bid. Just two years before I had been here in this same place, and I hated it, but this time I was on my way to one of the worst places a human being could be and be alive.

After I read Carrie's letter, I smiled. Her spirit was a refreshing one, unlike any I had felt in the last nine years. It was peaceful, it was joyful, and it was lively. Wanting to keep it close, I put the letter inside a book I was reading so I could take it with me on my hell-bound journey. Where I was headed was a deep dark place. I knew how absolutely insane population was, and I understood that in a place where the mentally ill and those transformed into savages by years and years of hard time are held captive, away from the rest of the population, have been abased to be the lowest of the low.

5

Lowest of the Low

He looks like you

He's a crook like you

But he don't walk and he don't talk and he don't act like you

He's not as sick as you because he knows what he is

And your shoe size is bigger than his

What's wrong with you

What ever happened to you

There was a time when no man would ever disrespect you

But this is how you want it to be

It saddens me to see a man get lonely

And submit to the pressures of the penitentiary!

—Yamini

Just as some prisons are harsher than others, some segregations are harsher than others, and it was the absolute worst in maximum-security facilities. The most violent, vulgar, rebellious, and in some cases influential prisoners were kept there. It was also the place where some of the guards' most brutal treatment of inmates happened. I thought I hated the county jail. This was far worse. This place would take a man to the brink of his sanity, because there were no limits to what some of these subhuman particles would say or do. Animals were cleaner in their behavior and in their impulses than some of these people. I was so caught off-guard by what I was seeing that the only reference I could think of for this conduct was ancient barbaric civilizations.

In prison, the mentally ill live among the inmate population, unless they are so violent or so detached from reality that they need around-the-clock care. These men cannot maintain normal prison life, so they are housed in segregation for a good part of their sentence. Their chaotic behavior was always a cause for disciplinary action, which made it easy for the administration to keep them isolated.

The day I arrived at segregation, I witnessed one of the most talked-about features of maximum-security seg. Low Down, an inmate assigned to do basic janitorial duties and other small tasks, was standing in front of a psychotic prisoner's cell and having a heated argument with him. Whatever the disagreement was about, Low Down was fuming. He collected all the thick mucus he could pull from his chest, spat on the man, and walked away, cussing him out. Later that evening, as he was mopping the gallery, Low Down got too close to the cell of the man he was arguing with and he whacked Low Down in the face with a "shit bomb" (feces and urine wrapped in plastic or napkin). The cell house went wild. Cheers and jeers echoed through the segregation unit for twenty minutes to celebrate this great accomplishment.

Feces and urine only come from one place. This means that the person who threw it had to either dig down in his toilet with his hands to pack both urine and feces in something until it filled or squat down and move his bowels directly into whatever he was using to throw. Next, he had to sit by the cell bars and wait for the opportunity to strike, which could have been hours. Every time he hears or thinks he hears someone on the gallery, he has to get himself ready to bomb. I've known men to spend entire days lurking in position by their bars, like Special Forces units, waiting to attack the person they're feuding with using one of these bombs. Is this not madness?

Not to be outdone by his nemesis, Low Down went to make a few bombs of his own. Revenge is a must in the penitentiary, and it has to be severe. When it was time to pass out the dinner trays, Low Down came with his arsenal and bombarded the man in his cell. The officers said it looked like an elephant with diarrhea was trapped in the room. Where Low Down got all that crap from is still a mystery. He was the janitor after all, so I figured that he'd been cleaning out toilets for hours, gathering ammunition.

This is all extreme. What increased the level of vulgarity was that Low Down boasted that he did something that I refuse to mention to the man's food. None of us wanted to touch our trays after that. I was angry that I had to question my only means of food and refused to eat whenever Low Down was working. Everybody hated him. He was a despicable character beyond belief that had the full support of the segregation officers. He did all their dirty work, and they loved and fed him.

The only reason I am sharing this with you is so that you understand the kind of men I had to deal with in prison. People often ask me why men who have served long sentences are so hard, speak so harshly, or are insensitive or unempathetic to other people's feelings. Well, what you are reading about is why. Prison is hell on earth. It is also a community—a society. If any of you have brothers, husbands, fathers, sons, uncles, or nephews who have been exposed to its environment for such a long time, they may have thinking and behavior that is compatible with a chaotic, abnormal culture beyond the reasoning and understanding of normal thinking people.

Because of the nature of my disciplinary report and the six months of segregation time, I was told by the officers that they wanted to "monitor my behavior". This meant confining me to a soundproof room, sealed with a steel door, that was issued to people whom the administration wanted to discipline severely. The mere fact that I was given one of these cells alerted me to the message I was being sent—and it still did not bother me. I preferred it to the open cells, and I preferred the peace and solitude that it provided over the loud chaos. The only drawback was that I could not socialize with anyone in the immediate area, nor could I pass or receive materials such as books, envelopes, or pictures, or do any trading of products, which is the bloodline of life in segregation.

I only had to do thirty days behind the door, so I spent the time reading and exercising. When the month ended, I was assigned to a regular cell and prayed that I didn't have to move into a small room with a maniac, which happened to me a few years before in the county jail. My prayer was not to be answered at that time.

Fifteen years is a long, long time to be imprisoned, and during that time I was blessed with fairly sane cellmates; however, I do not believe it is possible that anyone who has been in prison for so long has ever escaped the "Bug Celly." This is a cellmate with some sort of mental problem, and like all people, these men vary. Sometimes he has antisocial issues where he hardly ever speaks, and sometimes he is a compulsive liar. Sometimes he is a sexual deviant or a kleptomaniac, and sometimes he is a schizophrenic sociopath.

I didn't know what to make of my new cellmate, once I came from "behind the door." He was very calm on the surface, but underneath was a cold, dark creature who came out after a few days. When we first met, my celly was kind of cool and displayed a character that I was comfortable with, but the men who knew him best kept reminding me that it was smoke and mirrors, and that he was one of the most vulgar and hated men in the prison. Learning this news, I dropped my head in disbelief. For some reason I believed them, and I knew that I was in for a rough couple of months.

A few days went by without any problems, and I spent most of the time reading some of the books my new celly had. He had a collection of reading material that I'd been trying to get my hands on for years. I used to think that you can tell a lot about people by the books they read. My cellmate had books by Booker T. Washington, Eldridge Cleaver, Maya Angelou, and Martin Luther King Jr. He even had Nietzsche and Karl Marx and books on Harriet Tubman and General Hannibal. His personal library was impressive, but something didn't quite add up.

One day after lunch, I had just finished reading the book on Hannibal and enjoyed it so much I wanted to trade my celly something for it. I asked him if he'd read it yet and this fool told me he hadn't read the majority of his books; he just had them to check people on the wing whenever they held conversations that were historical. He said, "These chumps around here think they so smart; especially ol' boy down the way." After he said that, I looked him in his eyes longer than usual and saw madness. Here was a man who had books written by and about some of the most famous and influential people in world history, and he had absolutely no interest in their works or what influenced their thinking. His only interest was to show up and harass, criticize, and ridicule a few people whom he didn't like because they would bring intelligent conversations to the segregation unit.

After dinner chow one evening, my celly got into an argument with someone, which was the norm for him. He became angry with the guy and spewed the most venomous, vile, and vulgar language I have ever heard. The only reason I'm going to share this with you is because you really need to know how harsh many of the interactions with some of these people are—interactions that were inevitable and caused me great distress. If not for my need to warn our sons and daughters about the true reality of the prison experience so that they never have to experience it, I would take what I witnessed to the grave for fear of disturbing your minds.

When people spend significant amounts of time in segregation, they sometimes share certain small personal things with each other. I don't know what led to my cellmate's agitation, but knowing his character, it probably wasn't much. He had the type of personality that relished conflict and chaos. My celly knew how many young children the man he was arguing with had, and he targeted them with his vulgarities, telling the man how he would sexually mutilate his newborn and other young sons. My celly wasn't alone. Smunchie was another sick, vile, wretched individual whom he allied himself with whenever attacking men who wanted to have intelligent conversations. He was worse than my cellmate, and they fed off of each other.

Because I was so disturbed by what I was hearing, I sat up on my bunk and asked my celly who provided for him. I said, "Who cares enough about you to send you all this reading material or to put money in your account that allows you to purchase anything you like?" His answer was, his grandmother. I said, "She sounds like a wonderful, caring woman." He agreed that she was and that she was heavy into her church, so I asked him this question: "If this wonderful, God-fearing woman saw a live video feed of your behavior right now in front of her congregation, what would it do to her? Would she be embarrassed? Would she be shamed out of the building? Would she continue to support you?" He looked at me and glared, but he didn't say one word. It was fine with me because all I was trying to do was stop him from abusing my ears and my soul, and it worked; but not so for Smunchie. He was so despicable and contemptible that only God could reach him.

Once my cellmate ended his abominable verbal assault, Smunchie, the man he aroused to aid him in his malicious and venomous attacks, continued. For hours he described in detail how he would harm the children and other family members of the person he was talking to. Anytime anyone would intervene on his behalf and tell Smunchie to shut up or peacefully plead for his vulgarities to cease, he too was also met with vicious mockery. Everyone's response to this wretched individual was that he hoped to God one day to have the opportunity to meet him face to face. Smunchie had been targeted by all gangs, and if he ever left segregation in that prison, he was a dead man.

These are the types of behaviors and savage language that were held by some of the most despicable characters. They lived among us and were often disruptive, and there was nothing we could do about it. The only time I could have intelligent conversations was when these men were asleep. What also made the situation frustrating for some men was that the people who were the vilest would never leave their cells for recreation for fear of being attacked. Smunchie wasn't the only one who had a hit on him. There were a few others, and everywhere they went, they had to be escorted by guards. They even had to shower alone in a small cage with a single showerhead.

Like in general population, men in segregation are still allowed to go out to the yard, but only once a week for three or four hours. The seg yard was a group of four isolated chain-link cages covered with dull, rusted barbed wire; the yard looked like it was once one huge block. It was a kennel for men. The number of people outside at the time determined how many people were in each cage. The number was just divided by four, and men went to the cages they were told to.

I went to yard one day and wanted to play basketball, so I got close to the cage that had a rim that was in fair condition. Two of the other cages were just wasted space with torn-up blacktops, damaged backboards, and bent rims. I walked in and, as soon as I picked up a ball, Pete, a man I talked with often on the seg unit called me over to the fence. In a very low voice that only I could hear, he said, "Somebody is going to do something to your celly and I'm concerned that they could make a mistake and get the wrong person. You need to get up out that cell with that dude." I stood there looking at Pete for a moment, gauging the weight of his words. I understood him completely. "It's an easy mistake, Omar," he said in the same low but serious tone before walking away.

I threw the ball to the other guys in the cage, no longer wanting to play. My man had just dropped something heavy on me that made a lot of sense. You see, my celly and I looked a lot alike: we were the exact same height and close to the same weight, had the same skin complexion and muscle tone, and even wore our hair in the same low cut. It was easy for anyone to mix us up. All someone had to say was "hit the big, tall, light skinned cat in cell 47." But above all, of greater concern than the physical characteristics that he and I shared—which made it already difficult to tell us apart—was that he and I had the same name. His name was Omar, and everyone knew him by it. I was locked in a cage, in maximum-security segregation, in the worst place I had ever been in my life, with the some of the most despicable people I had ever known, and I came face to face with a person who had been transformed from a man into a savage and who looked like me and shared my name. I saw him as who and what I would become if I allowed myself to be influenced by this twisted and vulgar culture.

For a few days I thought deeply about the warning I was given. I stayed in the cell because I didn't have much longer to go, and by God's grace no danger came to me, nor was I threatened by any. Just thinking back on how my Lord communicated with me in that situation further encourages me to tell my story so that I may help keep as many young people stay out of prison as I can.

Another disturbing part of segregation was the vulgar sexual behavior. Prostitutes would intentionally catch tickets so that they could get relocated to seg, where they would rather be than deal with the inmate population. In seg they could perform the lesser sexual favors for more items purchased at the prison store. If you were wondering how someone could perform a sexual act while in segregation, where there is no contact with other prisoners, I have to give you another disturbing picture.

The cells are steel bars. If someone walks close enough to a cell, depending on the size of the arms of the person inside it, the person could reach out and grab whoever is walking by with both hands. This limited freedom of arm movement is just enough for a person to reach around into the cell next to him on either side with ease. It's how things get passed up and down the gallery. For the persons involved in what is called "sexual misconduct," it requires one person to be squeezed in the corner with his pants down and pressed against the wall while the other person reaches his arm around into the cell to perform the act. As shameful and vulgar as this behavior was, some of these men just didn't give a damn. They would get it on regardless of whether people were awake or not. It didn't matter. I hated that my cell was in close proximity to these guys. I was once in the middle of a conversation when all of a sudden . . .

Maximum-security segregation is so despicable a place that it could be sent into orbit and set on an asteroid, where it could float away from all living things. What can you say that may stop the behavior of mad men? What can you do except hate in your heart the vulgar actions of others when you cannot change the situation with your hands or move away? I believe anyone who has spent almost an entire generation in prison in the United States of America has had to live among and deal with some of society's most appalling and detestable exiles. I hated the continuous mental and emotional assault of its environment on me. It was fighting like hell to try to shape, mold, affect, and influence my mind and conduct.

Segregation pushed me to the brink. There were nights when I would lay there on my bunk, forced to listen to the most disturbing conversations. I would dampen tissues and stick them in my ears as deep as I could without harming myself so that I might block out as much sound as possible. Unfortunately, the noise level on those wings was extremely high. I could only block out so much. There are things I ask God to please remove from my memory so that I never have to remember them again.

Again, I really wish I didn't have to share some of these disgraceful conversations, but I really need you to understand how men are shaped, how they are hardened, how they have to deal with psychotic thinking and behavior. Prison is an intentional, unhealthy, perpetual tool of frustration used against anyone disrupting or breaking the rules of society. Like everyone else I paid a price, and that price was peace. My peace was disturbed and replaced with noise and clamor.

I continued to receive letters from Carrie, and they were always on time. I would get them every two weeks, which was just about when I had had enough of one of those lunatics. Her letters calmed me, not because they were sweet, but because they were intellectually stimulating and sincere. They were my momentary escapes from that insane asylum, and never before she entered my life had I watched and waited for the guards to pass out the mail like so many other inmates. If ever anyone was sending me money, pictures, books, anything, my attitude was "it gets here when it gets here." But now, I was excited, and I did my best to play it cool.

The day I got out of segregation I was so happy I smiled all the way to the property building where my belongings were kept. The morning was warm, the air was fresh, and the sun was on my face. I felt as if I was getting out of prison. It literally was the calm after a tremendous storm. I didn't even care about being in prison anymore. What I had just been through was so trying that everything else seemed easy. I was thinking this before I even moved to my new cell house. I read a verse in scripture that says when God wants to give mercy to his servants, He puts them through trials. I will never argue against that.

After getting my belongings I was escorted to the East Cell House in the back part of the prison. My cell was located on the third floor, so I climbed a couple of flights with all my property, walked up to the cage, and looked in. It was completely empty except for a sleeping man wrapped tightly in a sheet like a corn dog, with only his bald head sticking out. Something about this scene was very odd. I had cellmates before who had very few personal belongings because they had no one helping them on the outside, but this was a little strange. When the cell doors were pulled open by the officer, he sat up quickly, like a squirrel does when it hears a noise, and swung his legs over the side of the top bunk. Trying hard not to laugh, I said, "What's happening?" as he sat there with his legs swinging back and forth. I couldn't hold it in. I just started laughing in this stranger's face. My man was sitting there trippin' and I didn't care. "Whatever," I said to myself. "I've had worse."

As I unpacked my property and got settled in, my new celly, Duck, and I talked a little bit. As it turned out, he had been in prison for a long time and was one of those men with absolutely no family support and was left to fend for himself. All he had were a few letters from his grandmother, who still wrote him from time to time.

We talked for another half-hour, and I used the time to make an initial character assessment. All Duck could talk about or refer to was his guys, his gang. This man was in his early thirties and his topics of discussion were things a sixteen-year-old gangbanger talks about. I said to myself, "Ooh-wee—stick a fork in him; he's done." This stranger, whom I'd known for all of ninety minutes, began telling me way-out war stories and name-dropping well-known gang leaders from his area of Chicago, hoping to impress me. Many men in prison had this type of behavior. They would name-drop to make themselves appear to be somebody you needed to know.

Duck wanted me to believe that he ran with some of these people and had all these connections, and I didn't understand why. I gave him no indication that I was cut from that cloth. He had been in prison for at least seven years and didn't even have a $15 fan to cool himself off. The stories just didn't add up. I never told him that and didn't need to. Regardless of his untrue stories and needing to be a part of something, I kinda liked the guy. Yes, he was a bug, but he had a likable personality, which made living with him tolerable.

For six months I had to live in that cage with Duck, and for six months I heard nothing but gang-related stories. I tried the best I could to direct his mind, his thinking, to anything more productive than his norm. I offered him books and introduced him to meaningful television programs, but nothing seemed to work. So I just let him be. He was an adult who had made a decision to remain in his poor condition.

Duck was what is called a "nation baby." A nation baby is the type of person who always calls on or refers to his gang members for absolutely everything. He depends on them for support, companionship, and love. He is usually in the midst of all foolishness when trouble occurs, and many times he is the one to start it. Sadly, when this fool ages he is as dangerous an influence to young men as he is a pathetic sight to older men.

Being back in maximum security meant being surrounded by a different level of characters. The bugs were more violent, the inmates more delusional, and the gang members old as hell.

I knew a guy, whom I will name "Big Fella," who was the leader of his gang. At fifty years old and serving two natural-life sentences, Big Fella had a history of doing stupid, ridiculous things that was hard to comprehend for a man his age. He once had to spend time in segregation for having in his possession pictures and artwork of gang paraphernalia that he had someone create. Again, he was fifty, with grandchildren, and he was still having someone draw gang signs. Big Fella was caught trying to mail gang-related material home, knowing that all mail entering and exiting the prison is examined. He also knew that the mail of those who are considered a threat to security, a label he carried because he was a gang leader, was under a microscope as well.

When I heard the news, I said to the person telling me, "That's too bad." Not because he had to go to segregation for another idiotic reason but because this fool, who could hardly read or write, was the "authority" over his mob and had men obeying his commands. Over the years, the only thing that helped the followers of these types of men was their maturation. For some of them, the older they got, the more it dawned on them that they were following behind damn fools.

There is nothing as sorry, no sight more pathetic in prison, than the forty-year-old gang member. He is just a sorry, sad, worthless figure. He is the biggest threat to young men in the harsh prison environment. When I say "pathetic," I mean pitiful as hell. He has absolutely nothing else to do with his tragic life but try to influence other young men to behave like him. These young people, when they come to prison, this is what they're up against. They are up against the influence of this forty-, forty-five-, fifty-year-old gang member who, after all these years, still has nothing to show for his life on this earth.

Five months went by after leaving segregation, and they went by quick. One morning, out of the clear blue, an officer came to my cell bars and asked me if I wanted to go to the medium-security facility that was located a quarter-mile up the road. "Be ready to go in twenty minutes," he said. I didn't even answer. I just hopped up off my bunk and started unplugging cords and packing my things. Duck didn't have much property, so I completely split the food I had down the middle and also left him a fan and a Walkman. I wanted to leave him in a better condition than I found him, even though I couldn't get through to him.

All packed up and ready to go, Duck and I carried my property down the stairwell and out of the cell house. I was leaving maximum security forever, thanking God that He held me firm against the pressures that threatened my sanity.

6

A Comfortable Stupidity

The prison I was transferred to was literally around the corner. It was still on the grounds of the maximum-security facility; however, this section of it was for medium security only. For the most part, no one had more than than five years left to do on their sentence, whereas in maximum security you will need a calculator to add the time those men were serving. The procedures for transferring are the same throughout the state, so when I arrived, everything that I was asked to do I was already expecting. I was prepared for some officer with a bad attitude to act a fool with my property, and I also was prepared for other staff members to be annoyed with the new transfers as we came in. But to my surprise, it did not happen.

The guard shaking down property and the person issuing clothing were almost friendly. They were polite and respectful to us, and they were African American. Not since Joliet prison, six years earlier, had I seen this many African American officers. Instantly, I got a good vibe, because I wasn't used to this humane treatment. As I walked toward the cell house, I passed by officers who actually spoke to me or gave a nod that I recognized as a greeting to a stranger. One of them even said, "How's it going? Let me get you settled in." Regardless of the culture and race of these guards, I was shocked at the type of respectful, humane, decent treatment I was receiving. I walked into the cell house and it was the same. A female officer called me "sir" and told me exactly where my cell was without malice, disgust, or annoyance. "OK, I might be able to deal with this place," I said to no one in particular.

The cell house was designed exactly the same way as the X houses of the medium-security penitentiaries that I'd been in, so I had no problem finding my way around. When I walked into the dayroom carrying my property, a couple of men looked at me like I wasn't welcome. It made me a little uncomfortable but I kept moving because I recognized the look and didn't like it. A few years ago, before I matured, it would have been a problem. Looking around, I saw three young guys running around the wing, chasing each other like children playing outside. Another group was packed in the back corner of the unit, nodding their heads to a beat that someone was banging on a table while somebody else rapped. A couple of others were just lying around on a concrete slab that was supposed to be a bench right under the stairs.

The scene reminded me of the county jail, except in this atmosphere the men appeared to be in far worse physical shape. Many of them were slouchy and unkempt, and wore their clothes falling off. None of them seemed to care how they presented themselves. They looked like plantation slaves on drugs. They looked how people would look if they had absolutely no interest in learning how to read or write, and had no desire to ever work.

Finding my cell, I entered it and unpacked. My cellmate was a good, young nineteen-year-old kid named J. B., who had finally worked his way into the penitentiary by hanging out with people who didn't mean him any good. As the story always goes for this type of young man, when the police arrived, it was he that got caught. Because I saw so much of myself in him, especially in his route to prison, I made him the focus of my attention. I convinced him that nothing he wanted in this world was possible without an education, and that I would help him with his work if he signed up for GED classes. He did, and every evening we would go over anything he needed help with.

After a few weeks J. B.'s confidence grew, and he became more interested in reading material other than entertainment magazines and listening to music other than rap. When the day came for him to take the GED test, he passed it with ease, but I didn't let him stop there. "You gotta keep going," I told him. "It would be foolish to stop now. You can either prepare for your future and take college courses or run around the wing with theses clowns. Telling your family you've changed is not gon' get it. You have to show them."

Because J. B. had just recently passed the GED, his name was placed at the top of the list when the next school module began, and he received a notice in the mail for him to select his classes. He was now a college student. Like so many other young men who still have a lot of good in them, all he needed was a little push. He called his mother to tell her the news and he said she broke down in tears. For two years he had been running the streets with riffraff, getting involved in all kinds of crap, and after only five months in prison, he was in college.

Before I met J. B. I had been doing some serious contemplative thinking about my own life, my worth, and what my contribution to the world would be. Now I knew. At twenty-nine years old, it dawned on me that I had a gift that allowed me to speak to young men in a helpful and believable way that was easy to digest. But talking wasn't enough. Character is king, and before I ever spoke a word to any person about making improvements in his life, I made sure he knew me by my behavior first.

For weeks I didn't have much to do, so I socialized with the men on the wing. I played chess with a pretty good player every day, sometimes for hours, trying to improve my game. Spending as much time in the dayroom as I did, I became very aware of the behaviors and attitudes of most of the prisoners. The majority of the men in this small penitentiary were from the Southern part of the state and much poorer as a group than was the norm for prisoners. Individually there were not many people with TVs, radios, or other appliances. In comparison, the men from the Northern cities and towns had these material things, which created animosity and jealousies between the two groups. Their beef was that Chicago guys acted like they were bigger gangsters than they were and had a "you not as dangerous as me cause ain't nothing but killers in my hood" kind of arrogance. As foolish as it was, they felt like they were being disrespected and treated like lower-class thugs.

One afternoon during my daily chess match, an argument broke out a few feet away from me between a guy from Chicago and a guy from East St. Louis. They were arguing about which of them was the bigger criminal and which of their gangs was causing the most destruction in the land. They went on and on until I couldn't listen to them another second. I turned around and said, "Are y'all actually standing there arguing about which of your mobs have done the most devastation to your own communities, your own people, and your own families? Are y'all finally taking responsibility for destroying the neighborhood so much that the kids can't play?"

They didn't answer, so I continued. "If the two of you took the time to think about what you're talking about, you might piss your own selves off. You're arguing about whose raggedy-ass neighborhood is more impressive." It got very quiet, and everyone who was standing around supporting the dispute started walking away as if shamed. A short while after my statement to the group of young guys, the men on the wing treated me better than before. No one approached me with ridiculous behavior or spoke to me as if he had no sense.

As much as I wanted to hang with some of the younger guys, I couldn't, because all they could seem to talk about was drugs, drugs, drugs, and how many baby mamas they had. It was sad as hell. In fact, it was so sad, I gave up on them. I knew not to waste my time on people in a condition that severe. Their conversations affected me so deeply that I was inspired to write a poem, which I performed at a spoken-word show in the gym in front of a small audience of 150 people.

Ain't nothing wrong with selling cocaine
Pushing a product on the people that pimps the brain
You think I care because your mother's a fiend
Hell, I got champagne wishes and caviar dreams
Ain't nothing wrong with selling cocaine
You lames gon' stay out my business while I make my name
I'm gon' teach my son this game cus it's sweet
And hard-working family man ain't me
Yeah, I like selling that cocaine

It makes some y'all's daughters do some strange, strange things

Don't blame me cus the kids ain't fed

I didn't put a gun to your woman's head

And force her to spend the money that was for milk and bread

Gimme mine!

And don't be lookin' with those angry mugs

I thought we were supposed to be thugs

To look down on me is hypocrisy

Cus I know the true reality behind y'all's fantasies

$400 shoes on your feet

Talkin' about your kids got to eat

Six different baby mamas in the street

Looking for a fool they ain't seen in weeks

Keep it real

You're addicted to the lifestyle

And you're addicted to the fame

So what is so bad about selling a little cocaine?

$1,000 a day tax free

Man, to hell with what your family wants you to be

Get your sons some scales and your baby girls some short skirts

And teach all of your children that street hustlers don't work

They say that the property values in our neighborhood is a disgust

But we don't own naythin' so don't put that on us

Naw, not God, in the almighty dollar I trust

And by any means necessary is a must

Oh yeah, I see your baby girl; what, she's about sweet 16

Pretty brown eyes getting an appetite for those material things

I got her proud papa

I'm gon' keep your pride and joy laced in Dolce & Gabbana

Cause see, money don't need game

Ain't nothing wrong with selling a little cocaine

But don't get caught cause I'm in this for myself

So I hope you got enough sense to stack your wealth

My indictment better have one name on it and one name only

If not, then well, I feel for you, homey

If you think this here's about honor, somebody done told you wrong

Them people talkin' 40 strong before I ever come home.

Guilty! Damn, I think I'm gon' cry

Ain't nothing wrong with selling cocaine was all a big lie

I'm about to be a granddad; my daughter's pregnant; the father, too, just got indicted

The feds seized everything they own, and it killed my excitement

Now I'm locked away forever in this dreary, dismal penitentiary

Thinking about the billions and billions spent on technology

About how I was going to outsmart these government agencies

Without a college degree, a high school diploma, or a GED

I must be a damn fool!
—*Yamini*

The gym exploded into wild cheers that lasted for a couple of minutes. There wasn't an empty seat in the house, and as I stood there looking at the crowd I thought, "Ummm, OK." I wrote this poem because of the troubled thinking of many of the men in the audience and had no idea it was going to be accepted so graciously.

After I ended my attempts to reach some of those guys, I refocused on myself. I was given a job in the LTS department, where the staff was smooth and there were no other bugs working to disturb the peaceful atmosphere. Not only did the months fly by but it was also the most peaceful period of my imprisonment. I was in good health and so was everyone in my family. If only this prison had been closer to home. The almost 700-mile round trip was too much to ask anyone to visit, so I never did.

Distance was the greatest problem for maintaining any kind of family relationships. Men who were from small towns in the area of the prison had it better than others. They could visit with their loved ones on a weekly basis. Although the relationship may have been strained because of the man's imprisonment, it wasn't further burdened by 8-hour, 600-mile round-trip journeys that had to be planned like vacations. This was the reality for many prisoners—a reality that cut off any hope of attempting to manage a halfway decent relationship, especially if it was a romantic one.

My time left to serve was becoming less and less. Those fifteen years that I began with were now down to four, and it was time for me to make my way north, where I could receive visits from my loved ones and get the preparation for reentry into society that I so desperately needed. It was early in 2007 when I transferred to the prison where I would spend the remaining four years of my sentence. It was there that everything I had been through in the previous eleven years came full circle, and I was able to make connections of my experiences and give them the proper perception.

7

Almost Home But Not Really

When boys lose faith, they look to men to be their guiding light

When men lose faith, they look to death to end their painful fight

This destructive behavior of the young African American male is as dire as dire could be

With education on the rise along with self-employed enterprises, what truly is keeping a people from being free?

When boys lose faith, they close their eyes and lower their heads in shame

But when men lose faith, they walk out on their families, never to be heard from again

Is a man a man because he was born a male and stands about 6 feet tall

Or is a man the man who protects his family—loves, cares for, and supports them all?

What's crazy is . . . And this is really crazy to me

Because we can all agree on what a man should be

But if we take a look at the African American community

We will see the magnitude of this tragedy

So how do we fix it?

Easy!

We forget the blame games because those results have always been the same

And understand that a good portion of our people are suffering
from self-inflicted pains
Some say the problem is lack of money and education
But if that was the case
The descendants of slaves don't have a long history of either one
But at least our neighborhoods were safe
Maybe tough love is needed to get some form of peace to exist
Because many of our people behave as if they are moral-less
As for me,
I will continue to do all I can
But no longer will I hold the hand of a faithless black man!
—Yamini

Logan Correctional Center was as far north as I could get. It is in the middle of the state, and it was the first time since I left Joliet that I had been that far north. The staff wasn't too nuts, which made treatment more tolerable than any other place other than the medium-security facility that I had recently left. When I arrived, I went through the hated strip search and the frustrating property search, but without incident I headed straight to the housing unit.

The housing units were nothing like the X house designs that I have seen. These were all low-rise, one-story bungalows that were arranged like army barracks. Entering the building, I walked across a dayroom that was open spaced like a warehouse only packed with people. Many of them were sitting at tables playing a variety of games, talking on the phones, looking out of the windows, or watching a big TV. Because there was a shortage of chairs, many people held their conversations leaning against walls or sitting on the floor. It looked like a waiting room at an all-male clinic.

Walking to my cell, I went through a long hallway with a bathroom that was accessible twenty-four hours a day. That was new. It was the first time I had ever seen a prison layout in which the sink and toilet were not in the cells, and I was loving it already. No more smelling the filth of another person or having to hear his urine or feces plunge through the water all hours of the night.

Using my key, I walked into a cell approximately 15 feet by 10 feet, which is a fair bedroom size except for one thing—it had to be shared by four men. Damn! "I hope ain't no bugs in here, I said to myself. Scanning the cell quickly I saw that there was only one person in the room at the time. He was sleeping when I came in, saw me, said "wus up," and then rolled back over on his side, facing the wall and snoring again in seconds. I was nothing but another new celly.

Later that afternoon, after all my new cellmates were in the cell, I broke bread with them and cooked dinner. This was my icebreaker. Whenever I had a new cellmate, dinner was on me. It helped to eliminate problems from the jump and eased whatever suspicions that may have been whirling around in their heads whenever a new person moved in. Dinner was ramen noodles, summer sausage, cheese, crushed-up chips, and mayonnaise. I rolled the "dip," as the meal was called, in a tortilla shell and gave a soda pop and a candy bar for dessert to each of my cellies. It may sound disgusting, but believe it or not, it was always ten times better than eating that soy garbage that was being served in the chow hall.

After the officers came around and took a head count for the afternoon shift, I left my cell to use the phone and let my family know I moved closer to home. When I went out in the hall, there were at least twenty-five people huddled behind a barred gate that led into the dayroom, waiting on the officer to open it. I watched the scene closely, not knowing why everyone was hanging around pushing and trying to squeeze past each other to get to the front.

Opposite the cell house was the south wing, and another group of twenty-five men or so impatiently waited behind the gate for it to open as well. When the guard announced that the dayroom was now open, fifty grown men of all ages burst through the gates like racehorses in a full sprint to grab one of the few tables or chairs. People were arriving at tables at the same time, and tugs-of-war and snatch-and-grabs were often had, which led to arguments and fights.

Watching the mayhem in complete surprise, I saw two men arrive at a table at the same time, but both of them were claiming it. Because neither of these forty-year-old men would yield to the other, they both sat on it like a couple of first-graders so that neither one of them could use it. One of my cellmates told me that this converging on the dayroom happened every day of the year, Monday through Sunday, and nothing ever changed. Learning that made me think of the Bill Murray movie "Groundhog Day", where he woke up every morning and the same exact thing was going on.

As I got settled in, I noticed that a significant number of women worked here, and I knew that because of their presence, men were probably doing some stupid things. Over the years I've known really bad incidents to happen to both men and women because of their involvements with each other, and some of them were horrific.

In the state of Illinois, there are many female correctional officers who work inside of prisons. Many times, whether intentional or unintentional, they find themselves the object of the desires of thousands of inmates. Catcalls and other degrading and demoralizing remarks were said to her or among prisoners in regard to such a woman. There have been many times that I have been walking in a line of men going to or coming from somewhere in the prison when a woman walks by and instantly, guys go into detail about what they would do with her if they ever got the chance. Every time she steps out in the open or enters a cell house, she becomes a fantasy, a sex toy in the minds of many men. A great number of prisoners have been away from women for ten, fifteen, and twenty years and have thoughts and ideas about them that are twisted and perverted—thoughts that have been influenced and saturated by hardcore pornography books and magazines.

Once in a while, one of these women working in prison finds herself in a situation where she has gotten too close to a prisoner and ends up either in a secret relationship or even doing favors. These women spend many hours a day with direct contact with inmates and learn who they are—their stories, families, dreams, and aspirations. The reasons women find themselves in these secret relationships differ; however, those relationships can be very, very dangerous to a prisoner. I knew a couple of men who were involved in these situations, and neither of them ended well. They each got into flings with female officers, and one man was jumped on by other prison guards. The female officer wanted the fling to be over, and the inmate couldn't handle her ending it. He was shipped to another prison because she accused him of stalking her. Of course, she never admitted their involvement to administrators because she would have lost her job and could possibly have been prosecuted.

Another situation involved a volunteer who would come to the prison doing faith-based volunteering. After meeting a prisoner, the two of them formed a relationship and she was forced to resign. There was also another incident where a civilian female employee was bringing a prisoner penicillin because she had given him an STD.

The inmate population always knows which women will "go." It is gossip, prison news. Some of these women are extremely flirtatious, making them extra dangerous because other officers are aware of their behavior. A flirtatious woman's presence alone provides the possibility that some inmate may get lucky or "come up." But they almost always get caught.

There is the other type of woman who doesn't flirt, and she is just being her natural kind self. She is someone who is concerned about the welfare of a person who is being kept like an animal. Her warm, caressing, empathetic, and sympathetic personality is often misread by some person who doesn't understand women or care much about them, and sees her as if she has a romantic interest in him. However, because there are so many mentally ill men in prison, a sick mind misreads her and it puts her in danger.

Women, of course, are watched very closely for the most important reason—their safety. They could easily become victims of sexual or any other violent assaults. When a female officer accuses an inmate of something, whether it be verbal abuse or touching her inappropriately, that accusation will get him some serious segregation time, a serious beat down, or a new case.

Being separated from women for so long further removed from me knowledge about them that I hadn't quite understood to begin with. Coming to prison at such a young age ended any education on women I had learned up to that point just by being in their presence. Although I didn't know much, I saw how powerful an effect they had on some men. Some of them found themselves at a female officer's desk and in her face all day, smiling and giggling and behaving like thirteen-year-old boys. For hours they'd sit next to her, dry-snitching (talking about other people's business in a way that makes them guilty of something) and revealing character information about other inmates. To the population, such men are seen as "marks" or "ducks" and are not to be trusted. Oftentimes such a man finds himself in a very dangerous situation the moment someone feels that he is offering information on him.

The most troubling of all issues that women face is when they are viciously and savagely attacked. In my fifteen years I have known these incidents to happen in different prisons across the state.

One day, when most of the prisoners were out on the yard, a female lieutenant was brutally attacked in the cell house, and no one came to her aid for several minutes. She was beaten so badly that she didn't come to work for close to six months.

In another terrible incident, a female officer was running the a.m. medication line in the health care unit and was cussing out a man with mental illness from behind a locked door. She went to unlock the door to let another inmate in the holding tank where everyone was being held and thought she locked it behind her. The unstable man pushed on the door that he knew she hadn't locked, ran out to where she was sitting, and beat her bloody.

Female guards working in prisons are not soldiers or police officers. They are women from the local town or village who have a job and are many times assigned to a cell house full of powerful, aggressive, and perverted men. She is not carrying several different weapons that she can use to defend herself. Some of them, not all, carry mace. She just better hope the 250-pound goon she just sprayed wasn't close enough to grab her.

Getting the feel for Logan Correctional didn't take much time at all. Although there were some minor adjustments that I had to make, I had been in prison so long that each facility felt pretty much the same. Right away I wrote a letter to the school administrator to see what types of classes were being offered. For years I had heard about educational opportunity at this prison, which was another major reason I wanted to transfer there. The opportunity part was true, but none of the courses I needed were available, so I had to reconsider pursuing an associate's degree. Instead, I turned my attention to vocational studies and took Constructional Occupation, a course that taught me the basics of construction, wiring, plumbing, blueprint reading, and masonry.

I learned very quickly that Logan was a low-tolerance penitentiary for anyone who broke its policies, including the pettiest and most annoying ones. The policy that I and most all other inmates identified as the most aggravating is called "trafficking and trading." This translated to "don't give another prisoner anything, ever." On the surface it was supposed to alleviate debt created from prisoners borrowing merchandise from each other, but underneath it was an attack on basic human relations.

The reason for this policy is a practice among inmates called two-for-ones. This is a devastating interest rate that a person agrees to that obligates him to pay back twice what he borrowed for each item. For example, if I borrowed two packs of cookies, two bags of chips, and four noodles from the guy who is running "a store" (which is against the rules), in return I would owe him four packs of cookies, four bags of chips, and eight noodles. This type of borrowing can get very expensive and dangerous to someone who doesn't receive much help from the outside world. If he's late paying what he owes, many times his penalty increases, and most likely he will be threatened with violence.

A man named Li'l Chris once got a vicious beating for stringing along a group of gangbangers about when he could pay them. He kept telling them that his people were sending money that was either taking too long or never coming.

Some men had serious borrowing problems. They would always be on the verge of getting their brains stomped out and would have to find some way to pay what they owed. Watching men borrow so recklessly helped me to understand the financial institution. It taught me that when poor people who can't afford something go out and borrow money to buy what they want, they get into a deeper mess because they couldn't afford the thing in the first place.

I stated before that I've had well over a 150 cellmates, and one of those many different men was Caz. Caz borrowed and borrowed and borrowed. He would ask people for things like five packs of cookies, six pops, and a case of noodles, and have to pay back double per item; and it was breaking him. Every time he went to commissary he owed almost everything out, and after paying his debts he would sit on the stool in our cell with a "woe is me" look on his face. For weeks I tried to convince Caz to stop this reckless borrowing, but he just couldn't help himself.

Right after owing out everything he had, the week before, he did it again, but this time he couldn't stomach giving it all out. Guys were lined up outside our cell to collect their merch (merchandise). "Your celly is sweet," a young nineteen-year-old told me while carrying an arm full of snack cakes he had just collected from Caz. "Yeah, he's definitely candy," another person said who was standing nearby, waiting to collect what he was owed.

As he paid off his debts, my celly watched his groceries get lower and lower. Then he said, "That's it. Everybody else gon' have to wait. I ain't gon' starve again like I did last week." He left the cell to ask the last couple of men waiting to be paid if he could get them next week, because he was out. One of them agreed and left, but the other wasn't trying to hear it and told Caz to go get his merch. "Nope," said Caz, "can't do it this week. I got you next week." Suddenly, fwap, bap, crack, and slap sounds could be heard down the hall. It was going down, and I didn't intervene for a few reasons. First, it was a one-on-one fight between two men about the same size. Second, Caz told the man to his face he wasn't going to pay him, when he had the means to. He had to stop his excessive borrowing before it got him seriously, seriously injured. Also, after being in prison for twelve years, it was my experience that there was no single action, absolutely nothing, that humbled a man and adjusted his behavior better than a good old-fashioned ass-whuppin'.

Caz came back into the cell limping, exhausted, and looking beat up and crazy. With his heavy country accent he said, "That's it, I'm done. I'm not borrowing nothin' else" and plopped down on the stool.

It was the hardest laugh I ever had to hold in. I fought and fought and fought it until it went away, then I said, "Good. Too bad it came to this. If you need anything, just holla, but you need to pay your debts, because this problem ain't going away."

There were other times when a person's debt accumulated so much that he would be intimidated into giving up his TV, radio, headphones, beard trimmer, fan, or hot pot. Some men were losing everything they owned because they couldn't pay back what they borrowed from those vultures. It wiped them out. I had to bail out my celly so those wolves wouldn't seize his appliances and what little else he had.

The trafficking-and-trading policy was created to prevent what had happened to Caz from happening to everyone and was a rule in all prisons—a rule that says no prisoner can hand another prisoner anything. The problem was that the policy prevented us from sharing. Please understand the harm in this. Sharing is the most basic form of humane treatment, and in prison a great number of men are in desperate need because they don't have the family to help them survive. So I ignored the policy completely. It bothered me that this rule threatened me with a penalty for being charitable, kind, and neighborly in such harsh conditions as penitentiary living.

Because Logan was a medium-security facility, it was open to prisoner movement, which made possible every kind of nasty, foul, sexually related behavior led by the male prostitutes. Some of them were just as feminine as women, and some of them were just as masculine as men. Then there was the type that was in between.

A guy I will name D was in between. D was about 6 feet tall and 215 pounds with an athletic build. When he spoke, his voice, body language, and all other mannerisms were feminine, but when he played basketball or got involved in any activities that required him to be physical or a little aggressive, he was all male. I once saw him get into an argument on the basketball court with another man named Yobi. Yobi and D had a public on-again, off-again relationship that escalated violently when D reached up and slapped Yobi's taste buds loose, knocking him to the ground.

Another time, D called a young guy out who was talking trash to him. He invited the youngster into the shower, a place people would go to fight, and knocked him out cold. He became the prostitutes' hero, their champion, and it was because of his show of aggression that he began to "get outside his body." This term is given to a man who has become arrogant or big headed, usually after winning a fight or two. D started barking (making idle threats) at some of the younger guys who were always targeted for mistreatment by anyone with an agenda. There was an unwritten rule that was followed by most prisoners, and that rule was "leave those prostitutes alone." The young guys loved to aggravate them, so D used to beat them up, and it made him bolder and bolder.

D, along with everyone else who often got into fights, was very selective in whom he was going to try. One day he tried the wrong person and got the hell beat out of him. It was one of those feel-good whuppin's too, because D had become a bully. The only reason he lasted as long as he did was because prostitutes were ignored when they got to acting crazy.

You see, arguing with a male prostitute made a man look bad because (1) whoever gets whupped by him is going to have to live in shame, shame, shame and will be clowned for years. Every time such a man gets upset or gets tough with anyone else, he will be reminded of his beat down by everybody. And arguing with a male prostitute made a man look bad because (2) arguing with prostitutes was something that only happened between tricks or lovers or when there was a payment dispute.

A masculine guy who messed with prostitutes was a little different. He was the type of man who would have a relationship just because he didn't have anything else to do. Many of these men had wives and children and didn't have any emotional attachment to the man he was flirting with. He was just in it for the sexual pleasure.

One man, Shuckey, was pimping a couple of prostitutes. He was very boastful in how he did his work, too. I could not stand this person. I hated everything he was and stood for and made it my business to not be in the vicinity he was in. Everything that came out of his mouth was so disturbing it aggravated my spirit.

The type of prostitute who was the most disliked was flamboyant, loud, obnoxious, and annoying. One day, while I was sitting at a table in the dayroom reading a book, two prostitutes sagging their pants and showing off their butts, in case anyone was interested, began having a conversation a few feet from me. The dayroom was crowded and there was no place else to sit. Because they wanted the table I was sitting at, they began to talk about who they thought was cute and some of their recent sexual activities. They went into detail about their exploits, knew I would not be able to stomach their conversation, and anticipated me leaving, which I hurried up and did. They won. They almost always won.

I hated prison. Hated it!

The most troubling way of all penitentiary living was living on alert like a soldier in enemy territory. Everyone was on alert every time he stepped out of his cell. Some men had been injured so many times that their behavior became extreme paranoia.

J. D. was a man who had been involved in too many prison fights and been present in too many places that "went up" (a riot). He had been hurt so often during these senseless explosions that he walked down the hallways with his shoulders brushing against the wall, just in case something went down. He did this to make sure no one was ever behind him. Whenever he was in the dayroom, he was either leaning against a wall or had pulled a table into the corner. J. D. also had a serious problem he was dealing with. He had messed up his gang's box, their commissary merchandise, and it had a large amount of items missing that were unaccounted for. Because he was the one responsible for it, he had a violation coming, and it was going to be brutal. It was sad to see him live that way. That is no way for a human being to live.

A few months passed by and my cellies came and went. Some of them were good guys and others were characters I just wanted to go away. Unfortunately for me, I went through a period during which characters just kept rolling in.

The first character, Milo, was a young guy in his mid-twenties who had been bouncing around from town to town, mesmerized by the drug game. The man was completely in love with it. He also was a habitual liar. I just couldn't get the truth out this dude. He would forget the lies he told so much it made talking to him pointless. By the time Milo was done with me, I didn't know who he was, where he was from, how many kids he had, or if his parents were alive or dead. Depending on whom he was talking to, his story changed. I ignored him because I'd seen his kind before; however, I was more concerned about another condition he had. Milo was a cutter, and on both his arms were healed slice marks that showed where he'd been cutting himself whenever he got extremely upset.

One day Milo stormed into the cell frustrated because some buddies of his were calling him out on his lies in front of everybody. He paced the room for a while, then sat on a stool, rocking and pulling at his hair. In low murmurs like a twelve-year-old boy, Milo began whining about how badly he wanted to go home, how much he hated this joint, and how these guys were going to make him do something crazy. I sat up on my bunk and pulled my headphones off, giving him my full attention, not saying anything, but watching. I was trying to give him time to cool off, but he kept rocking and mumbling. After a couple more minutes I asked, "You not gon' do something to somebody that's gon' get you more time than you have, are you?" I knew he didn't have the courage to try anyone, but I made it sound like he did.

"Naw, man," he said. "I'm just so sick of this stuff. Sometimes I just don't want to live no more. I just be wanting it to be over with."

I didn't know that Milo was that unstable and had no idea how to deal with this kind of situation. Because I thought he was at the edge of the cliff, I eased him into a conversation about the things that excited him most—women, rap music, and other people's money. After an hour and a half of talking about strippers, whack rappers, and all the money athletes and entertainers had, Milo calmed down and was back to his normal lying self. It was like the whole thing had never happened.

For a few days I tried talking him into getting some help with his condition, but nothing came of it. A short while later, he was told by the officer that he was on transfer to another prison. Being in a cell with him had lasted only two months, and like so many people who entered my life, Milo was gone as quickly as he had come.

Another cellmate I had to deal with while I was dealing with Milo was a thief. Pops would steal anything that wasn't chained down and padlocked. Worst of all, he stole from the people he lived with. That's a no-no. That was a thing that could get all a person's teeth kicked out his mouth and was the primary reason cellmates got into fights with each other. There had to be some kind of trust with the person you lived with, if not with anyone else. The only things that stopped my other cellmates from crushing him were me and his health condition. Pops was in his mid to late fifties, had a bad heart, and was on nitrates and a bunch of other stuff. If ever he got too scared or too excited, something bad could happen to him. Still, he had to live in our cell on threats—my cellmates had to threaten the hell out of him all the time.

Whenever I didn't know how to handle a situation, I would always ask someone who I thought had a little sense. In this case I went to a friend named Dollar and told him what had been going on. He listened and said, "Y'all let that go down for too long. The man is stealing in your face, which makes you a better man than me or a fool, because I would have been slapped him under the bunk!" Well, I couldn't do nothing with that advice.

Because word travels fast regardless of what it is, it wasn't long before most of the cell house knew what was going on. As was to be expected, "kick his tail" was everybody's solution, but it wasn't mine. However, Dollar was partly right. I did let it go too long. Pops was stealing from me too; I just ignored it. His behavior was that of a homeless person, and deep down I thought that was the case. The items he was taking were few, and unless it got so bad that I had to address it, I let it happen. It was just a tough situation for me to deal with, and it all centered on his health. My other cellmates weren't having it, though.

B. G., my third celly, whom I was thankful for because he was as smooth as they got, was tired of the old man going into his property box and taking what little he had. He got to a point where he no longer cared about Pops's health condition and wanted to hurt him, and it almost happened.

B. G.'s favorite chips, which he was saving for the Bears game, came up missing, and he was fuming. "I got something for your boy when he gets in," he told me.

"Be cool, bro," I said. "I need somebody sane in here with me or else I'm gon' bug up. I got some chips. We're giants and that's a small matter."

"All right", he said, "but I bet that's the last time he takes something from me." Moments later Pops waltzed into the cell like none of us were aware he was stealing real good. As soon as the door closed, all 260 pounds of B. G. hopped off the top bunk and thudded onto the floor, right in front of the old man. Eyes screaming bloody murder, B. G. pressed his forehead hard against Pops, mashing bone against bone, and gave him a final warning. The old man was so scared his entire body started trembling. He lost all the air in his lungs so fast he had to sit down or collapse. I got nervous because I thought his heart was giving in, and had to intervene. The one thing I didn't want was

Pops passing out, or worse, having a heart attack, in our cell. He was so afraid of B. G.'s intimidation move that he went to internal affairs and told them he was being threatened by us all and wanted to move. IA granted Pops his request to leave the cell, and soon after he left, officers began to raid the cell house regularly.

In Logan, as in many other prisons I've lived in, there was a person, or a few people, who continuously gave information to internal affairs that wasn't even worth telling about. I don't mean the major issues that prison officials sees as threats to the safety and security of the institution, like drugs, alcohol, or the manufacturing of weapons, but the smallest, most nitpicking things. For example, there is a rule that states no person can be inside a cell that they were not assigned to. The informant would inform internal affairs that there were men hanging out in cell's that they didn't belong in when those same men may have been invited by those who do.

Kango, a celly of mine, was in his buddy's cell watching a game. He didn't have a TV and didn't want to sit and watch it in the dayroom with all those clowns. Working on a tip, a lieutenant snuck in the back door of the cell house and went straight to the cell Kango was in, handcuffed him, and took him to segregation. Somebody petty snitched on him.

Another time, a friend of mine was taking a shower after the allowed time because too many people were trying to get washed up after a late gym. He waited until it cleared out and jumped in. The officer in the cell house didn't know or he would have written the ticket himself. An hour later, working on a tip, a different lieutenant came to his cell, read the name of the prisoner he was looking for, cuffed him, and took him to seg.

Another friend of mine was cooking a meal for a few of us on his birthday using a hot pot that was rigged to make the water boil. Rigged hot pots are considered contraband, and although no seg time is attached to it, C grade and loss of commissary shopping is. After we ate and the cell was all cleaned up, an officer came to his door, went directly to his property box, took out the hot pot, and left. He came straight for it. He didn't search the cell and he didn't ask which box was his. He had detailed information on the hot pot's location.

This type of dime-dropping was so petty that it was hard for men to stomach it, hard to understand why someone would do it. Whoever the person was, he was helping the administration punish us for basic human interactions and any courteous or kind relationships we may have had with one another. Whoever this person was, he was the most hated man in the joint, because he disturbed the everyday lives of people in prison and had men looking over their shoulders before they gave a hungry man a few crackers.

Because cellmates come and go so often, Milo, Big Guy, and Pops had moved on, and I had a new group of people: Smash, a buddy of mine I knew from the county jail; Billy, an eighteen-year-old white kid from one of the local towns; and Roger, a despised and disgusting human being convicted for molesting minors under the age of eleven. Roger was a sick, perverted old man who did not watch any sports other than the Little League World Series and high school boys doing anything. He would even watch the reruns of the games, excitedly stalking the young boys. Another favorite show of his was Are You Smarter Than a Fifth Grader?

I figured out he was watching children when late one night I saw him licking and sucking on a summer sausage like a freak while watching his kid programs. Seeing how excited he got, electricity shot through my body and I hopped up and stormed out of the room for fear of reacting. It was one of the most disturbing moments that I had in my entire prison sentence, and maybe in my entire life, because I had never witnessed a person get aroused when watching children. I had to be very careful with Roger too, because he worked in officers' kitchen and became very friendly with the staff of the prison. I'm sure they knew what he was convicted of because he was handling their food, but once I knew he was the kind of person who preyed on our babies, I couldn't live with him any longer.

The next day, I told my cellmates what I had seen the night before. Billy was shocked and said he always thought Roger was kind of weird. Smash was not shocked, though. Very nonchalantly he said, "Roger sleeps naked!"

"What?" I yelled back. In our cell, Roger was always the last to go to sleep and slept on the bunk under me. Smash and Billy were on the bunk on the other side of the room and could easily see down on the child molester's bed. Continuing his report, Smash said two nights ago, just before seeing what I saw, he saw Roger completely naked and creeping around the cell. He said he jumped up and asked Roger what the hell he was doing and his answer was he just wanted to ask Billy a question and then ran back over to his bunk. That's when I knew this freak had to go. He had a sickness, and I just thank God that I didn't see him in that room naked. That would have been it for me. I would have lost it all. A couple of days later, Roger was so uncomfortable with living with us that he requested a move to a different cell. His stay there was short but memorable.

Roger moved into a two-man cell with Dave, a young man who was taking many different kinds of psychiatric medications. Because Roger was sick and disturbed, he continued his antics of flirting with young men to see if they were interested in him.

Dave was very uncomfortable with Roger's behavior but was a soft-spoken kid with his own mental problems and never told anyone what was going on in the cell.

One night Roger got completely naked, sat on his bottom bunk, and shaved his private parts while Dave was on his top bunk watching TV. Unaware of what was going on under him, Dave looked over the side of the bunk and saw Roger with his razor in his hand. Dave went berserk! Screaming and yelling, the mentally and emotionally unstable young man broke the glass on the long fluorescent light that was attached to the ceiling in the cell and began cutting at his veins. With blood squirting everywhere, Dave burst out of the cell and ran down the hallway, into the dayroom, and up to the officers' desk. He was admitted to the health care unit and placed under around-the-clock watch to make sure he no longer wanted to hurt himself.

Later that evening, Roger was feeling bad that he had pushed Dave to a suicide attempt. He gathered the remaining shards from the broken light and, like Dave, he too cut at his veins. Roger, however, made a serious attempt to kill himself. When the third-shift officer came on duty and was making his rounds, he saw Roger lying on his bunk in a pool of blood, trying to bleed out. Damn!

Not long after Roger tried to take his life, another man did. Krill was a young white man from one of the neighboring towns with a history of dealing drugs. A couple of guys who knew him from the street said that his parents weren't worth a damn and that he had a younger sister whom he practically raised on his own. Krill decided he wanted to move drugs in and around the prison and was using his sister in his operation. They were caught shortly after they began, and she was charged with the serious crime of bringing drugs into a penal institution. Krill was so overwhelmed with the guilt of being responsible for getting his little sister caught up in his life that he committed suicide while in segregation, leaving the only person he cared about to face the charges alone.

My living arrangements forever seemed to be psychotic, because at least one of my cellmates was always nuts. This cycle went on and on and on, all while I was trying my best to hold onto my sanity. By this time, I was in my early thirties and had a good grasp of my faith, so it was easier for me to deal with some of the psychotic episodes that my cellies and others would have. In continuing to help whomever I could deal with in the madness of penitentiary survival, my path crossed with a celly who was dealing with a different type of harmful influence.

Hank, a young, white, twenty-five-year-old crystal-meth-head from Southern Illinois, was a fighter. Every time I turned around, he was either in the hallway or the bathroom fighting. He never backed down because he was not afraid of people, which made a white-supremacist group target him. They wanted Hank to be a part of their team because they would have somebody who would fight African American or Hispanic men without fear.

A couple of the white supremacists began hanging around our cell and introduced a few women to Hank to pen-pal with. Knowing that these snakes were using the powerful appeal of female companionship to lure him in, I said to Hank, "I like you. You're a good dude, but these racist bigots want you on their team. They know you and I hang out, and they never said a word to you until you started winning a few fights. So, if you want them as your friends, then we can't kick it no more."

Hank was very comfortable in our cell and didn't want to leave it. I was always generous to my cellmates and made our cell a place of peace and relaxation, away from the penitentiary madness, as best I could. My cellies and I would have intelligent discussions and meaningful conversations that we all enjoyed. They couldn't talk like this with their friends because their buddies weren't interested. We watched the news and then discussed what we thought was going on around the world and what we thought were the problems of education, politics, and people. We also discussed gang problems in the cities and their influences on young people regardless of their race, so when those white supremacists started coming around, our other two cellmates and I told him to choose friendships.

I reminded Hank of Richie, a young guy we both knew, who hung out and played cards, baseball, and even ate dinner with his African American buddies. As soon as a supremacist group wanted him with them, they gave him gifts, had women come visit him, and had him working out with them. They pulled Richie in and transformed him so fast that he shaved his head and sold all his rap music. When the white supremacists were disbanded and separated, Richie was on his own again and tried to come back to the people who had befriended him first. He was met with aggressive resistance and alienated, and he had to live in seclusion. Every time he came out of his cell to the public areas, he was cussed out viciously.

Hank, on the other hand, was a different kind of man. Although he was not a racist, he did enjoy the company of other white men, as he should have. Those were his people and he shared a common ethnic experience with them. The problem was that Hank did what so many young people do with gangs. He hung out with them and was seen as a supporter in their cause. As much as I hated to, I had to cut him loose for the associations he had chosen over good people with good sense. It was easy for me to recognize because I did the same thing as a teenager.

Many good things were going on in my life as my sentence wound down. I graduated and received a certification in my constructional occupation course, which was an accomplishment that I was very proud of. For men in prison, if they have the drive and the self-motivation to sign up for classes and pursue any type of education that is available, they will, at the very least, have a foundation from which to jumpstart their educational careers when they are released.

The one thing I am most grateful for from being in Logan was the opportunity to congregate with a community of believers. Every Monday we met for our discussion group, and on Fridays we fulfilled our religious obligations with prayer. We became a family. We ate together, exercised together, kept each other company; we helped each other when we were in need and valued peace, education, and meaningful conversations. We treated each other with decency and dignity, and above all, the inmate population recognized and respected us for it. Men called us brother because from us, they got a brother's treatment.

Though it was always dangerous, many of us would intervene in conflicts before they got to the point of no return, knowing that in a volatile environment such as a prison yard or cell house, a situation could escalate instantly. We also had good relationships with men of other faiths and played sports and board games together, and ate dinners with each other. We thought it was the best example of how to conduct interfaith relationships between men believing in the Creator of the

Heavens and Earth. It truly was a shield and a healing for those of us who were sincere.

The guards, however, were hot and cold. Some of them respected us, while others hated what we stood for. To these types it didn't matter if we were lawless or honorable. We were convicted felons and deserved whatever punishment we got. Their hatred for us was more an annoyance than anything. With their spiteful attitudes and petty behaviors, they would lie, saying that service was cancelled for the day or refusing to announce over the speaker system that the line for service was leaving. Movement throughout the prison was escorted by officers, and when that line came to the cell house and you missed it, that was it.

My life had progressed completely, and I resumed my study of scripture. Although I loved the man that I became, I didn't run around preaching and quoting verses that I didn't fully understand myself. I was not going to be the guy who read something in his holy book that touched him deeply and couldn't wait to go tell it. I knew quite a few men like that. They wouldn't be away from their former street associations but for a couple of months and would be on the young guys about their faith and behavior. It never went over well.

A man named Vaughn would always storm away in frustration after talking to the young guys because they weren't trying to hear nothing he had to say. To them, Vaughn was just another person who claimed to have found God, but nothing in his character or speech said believer. One day, after another failed attempt, I caught up with the frustrated man and said, "Your heart seems to be in the right place, but don't nobody know you like that. Just a couple of months ago you were talking about sticking up a dice game. That's how they still see you."

Another character, the Prophet, was doing way too much. No one could talk to him without him quoting scripture every two minutes. One day, I was watching a football game and saw a player get crushed. I asked Prophet if he saw the hard hit, and he went straight to chapter and verse, describing what went down. I said, "All right man; I'll holla at you," and hurried up and moved on. If it was any other person I probably would have appreciated his attempt at making a connection between scripture and the world we live in, but because this was how he always responded, I quickly ended a potential conversation I didn't want to have. The game was on, and he was trippin'.

The other guy I definitely wasn't going to be was the type who was so nice and so in love with his faith that everything was pleasant and wonderful, and the sun was always shining and birds chirping. I didn't get this type of man. We were in prison, and my eyes and ears gave me a different reality. Many of these men here were hardened and had very little faith in anything.

Speaking the typical language of religion was pointless. They needed a man from among themselves whom they'd watched for years make a sincere transformation and did so with courage and integrity.

I was blessed again to be given an opportunity to be one of the leading men who shared what I understood about our faith. My approach was basic: treat people how you want to be treated. That didn't need a whole lot of preaching, which was cool because nobody wants to be preached to. People were too busy trying to figure out when someone was going to send money so they wouldn't starve.

Time was moving at light speed, and I began to get a little nervous. I had one year remaining on my sentence, and there were some things I had not yet accomplished. I never finished my associate's degree, and it gnawed at me on a daily basis. I thought I needed something more than a certificate to show for fifteen years of imprisonment, but academic classes were still scarce. Feeling the pressure of what I thought wasn't a good enough transformation, I sat in the dayroom with my buddy Deal to tell him what I was going through.

Before I could get one word out, a crowd gathered near us to watch something that was taking place. I didn't know what was happening because I didn't sense any tension in the air, which is extremely thick whenever something serious is about to go down. Looking closer I saw two men standing face to face, showing all their teeth and snarling like wolves. One of the men was probably the most well-known bug in the joint. He was on every psychological medication possible. Seconds later they started barking at each other like pit bulls. Deal and I looked at one another in complete disbelief. "Uh-uh, nope," he said. "This ain't happenin."

I stared at him for a long moment, leaned in close, and whispered, "I just wanna go home. I just hit my limit."

At the time, I had been writing a journal on my last days in prison, and when this happened I got up, went to my cell, pulled out my pen and pad, and wrote down exactly what happened and how it happened so that I would be able to tell people forever and ever about the goings on in prison.

I wrote:

Because there are very few mental-health facilities available for people who need them, those who truly need psychological assistance are sent to prison instead for their crimes. There is a large population of men in prison who should be receiving some form of psychological treatment. These men are mixed with the general population. Some are violent, some are meek, and others are sexual deviants.

There is a man here who I do not believe is on any psych meds who at 52 years old barks like a guard dog and is proud of his closely sounding resemblance. You better not tell him he doesn't sound like a pit bull. I'm just happy that at 52 years old he's finally found his hidden talent. Maybe he has enough sense to try and market this great skill or start his own security company. All he has to do is hang out in someone's yard and every time a stranger approaches bark at them. I guarantee you they would run away from that property. I know I would. I'd be thinking that these people living in this house must be insane. Bark on brother with your barking ass. Lord, thank you for allowing me to remain sane. It could have been ugly. May peace be with you all who have kept your sanity through this dark, twisted nightmare.

I never told Deal what was on my mind because I forgot. Those two fools made me lose my train of thought. I got up from the table and headed to my cell because I had had enough crazy for one day. Walking through the dayroom and entering the hallway, a nauseating breeze crept out of the bathroom a few feet away and slapped me in the face. Not really wanting to, I couldn't help but go look in the bathroom to see why it smelled so bad. Peeking in, I saw wet turds plastered to the walls in both the shower and sink areas. It looked like there had been a manure fight. The bugs used to do stuff like that, and I could not help but wonder if those two lunatics who were just barking at each other had something to do with this. Then again, who knows? There were quite a few bugs living in the cell house.

There once was a mystery man who would take dumps and then scoop up his mess and plop it on the top shelf above the mirror for everyone to see. Of course you already know it sat there all day, because no one wanted to be the person to clean it up. Other times people were urinating in the sinks and on the floors and walls. The officers and other staff had their own private bathrooms and didn't use ours, so it wasn't payback against them. The issue was that many men had moral and mental problems, or were so angry about being in prison they didn't care that the bathrooms belonged to us.

Living with so many nasty, selfish people always created serious hygienic problems with public bathrooms, because scrubbing the toilets was the most hated assignment in the penitentiary. No one wanted to clean and wipe down stalls of urine, and feces, and blood, and mucus and any other disgusting, stomach-flipping, unbearable things to look at or touch. Who wants to clean a bathroom after two hundred people who didn't give a damn?

Because I couldn't stomach it, me and a couple of other men voluntarily rotated among ourselves to get the bathroom clean for the cell house. People respected us for that. They appreciated and respected us for it; however, they weren't going to clean that mess up, and we had to forget about asking for help.

Doing my best to live like a human being was harder than it was supposed to be, and I was getting tired of cleaning up behind men who behaved like savages. One evening as I was mopping, I saw a few drops of blood on the floor. Already annoyed because whoever was bleeding hadn't taken the time to clean up after himself, I noticed that these were not isolated drops of blood but a trail that led out of the bathroom and down the hallway. No sooner had I begun cleaning it up than the officer who was working the cell house came around the corner and saw it as well. He followed the trail to the cell it came out of, opened the door, and went in. I kept mopping the floor until I ended up at the cell where the door stood open. Looking in the room, I saw that a man on the top bunk, curled in the fetal position, was beaten so bloody he looked like a lump of flesh. The officer called his name several times, but he was so out of it he couldn't respond.

Immediately the guard called for a medical emergency, and when the nurses arrived, the unresponsive man was rolled out in a wheelchair looking like he had been in a motorcycle accident without wearing a helmet. The cell house was put on immediate lockdown and placed under investigation for the incident, and again I found myself sitting in internal affairs being questioned about what I knew. The wing officer told the lieutenant that he saw me mopping up blood, possibly attempting to cover up what had happened. I just knew I was in for a long next couple of days.

To my surprise, it didn't take much to convince the guards that the only thing I was doing was cleaning up a dirty bathroom. The internal affairs officer believed me, let me go, and said, "You might want to stop volunteering." As it turned out, Town, a big ol' strong dude bench pressing well over 400-pounds snapped in the cell and beat his celly mercilessly. I never found out what went down between them that caused the ferocious attack; I just kept it moving and filed it away as one of those things that happens in the penitentiary.

With no more school available to take in the short time I had remaining, I completely turned my focus to the younger guys who still had a lot of good left in them. Their biggest problem was they didn't have anything to do. Wanting to fill this void, a friend and I created basketball, board-game, and card-game tournaments. Sometimes the contest took all day, and whenever a person was eliminated, many young guys would still hang around and watch to see who won. To make sure we got full participation out of as many people as possible, we offered a pillowcase full of commissary to the winner. It turned out to be a good plan because many of the young guys were too busy with the tournaments to be running around like loose cannons, even if it was for just one day. Those times were always days of peace and enjoyment, and almost everyone appreciated it.

Of all the ways I was trying to help young guys to be human, the thing I enjoyed most was having meaningful, intelligent conversations with men who were not used to it. We had to have rules though: (1) No talking about how well-off people are for selling drugs; (2) no disrespecting women; and (3) no glorifying any harmful behaviors of any kind. I told the guys, "Those types of conversations can be had anywhere around here, so ain't no need in us doing it too."

Listening to young men sincerely express themselves opened my mind up to how talking about these issues was therapeutic. I didn't know if it was the absence of drugs and alcohol that brought some of them back to life or if it was someone showing them he honestly cared and didn't want anything in return. I had mixed feelings about which young guys to pick, because I wanted to help them all. The problem was that some of them had issues so deep they needed clinical care.

I was on my way to the chow hall for lunch, and two young men were in line in front of me, walking side by side. One of them was angry because he couldn't get his grandmother and his children to come visit him. They didn't want to visit their father on Father's Day. Speaking to his buddy, he cussed out his grandmother and his babies for not wanting to see him, calling them all kinds of vulgar names. My heart sunk knowing that this young man was their father and that the chances were great that he would never be in their lives, and if so, to what detriment.

Normally I don't get involved with people's conversations because it's not healthy, but this time I felt compelled. To the young man who was trippin' hard I asked, "How old are you?"

He said, "twenty-three."

I said, "I heard you say you have kids. You're too young to have older children, so they must be babies."

He replied, "Yeah, they're four and six, but they be on BS!"

"BS," I said. "You know today is Father's Day, right?"

He said, "That's why I'm pissed off. My stupid grandma won't bring them up here on Father's Day. Talkin' 'bout they don't want to see me. That's all right. F 'em then! I ain't got but a few months anyway. They gon' be beggin' me to kick it when I get home!"

Listening to his tirade and observing his animated body language, I was developing a strong dislike for the young man, but after his last comment I wanted to beat him up. Instead, I shook my head and shut my mouth, knowing that another word from me may have caused a fight.

Of the many troubling issues with young men in prison, the fact that so many of them are desensitized to seeing people in pain is the most frightening. Before lil dude's Father's Day rant, I had never heard someone that young speak of his own children so callously and heartlessly. Other youngsters were zombies, wandering around the prison lost, targets for the officers and older inmates looking to abuse them. They were so painful to watch because they were impressionable and had been under the influence of the street life and gangs, as well as all other harmful influences from their home environments.

Some of them were so heavily influenced by their gangs and whatever else they were raised around that they would kill one, two, three people. They were so desensitized about it that they deserved life in prison, if not worse. I really hate to say that. They don't see themselves as murderers or cold-blooded mass killers.

I had a conversation with a young guy named Marco, who loved the hell out of his gang. The topic came up about all the killing in the street when guys go out and do hits for whatever reasons, or as he put it "cats getting they wigs pushed back." I said, "Whoever does this is a sendoff man. If that is your behavior, if you go out and kill somebody because someone told you to, you are a sendoff man." The youngster stood there as if annoyed but didn't say anything, so I continued. "Whatever happened to doing something to somebody who did something to you?" I asked. "What if, in the streets, guys only did things to people who did something to them? If that was your answer, then it would make sense. If your answer was, 'I did this because he did that,' then people could probably wrap their minds around it. Not that they would support your decision, or agree with your response, but to just go out and kill people, to shoot up homes and crowds, is cowardly, mindless crap that no one understands. And because it's so devastating to human life and to our society, the only reactions that lawmakers have are extreme ones."

Marco said, "Omar, all of the guys out there that are part of this thang are guilty. If they plugged, they've done some stuff to people because that's how they live. This is how we get down and ain't none of us innocent. Some of them guys in them crowds probably done got down on somebody else."

In a calm, collected, but serious tone, I said, "Damn, y'all just guessing what somebody probably did somewhere and go spray the block because those guys over there probably did it! Are you serious?"

He said, "That's how it is, and if they don't like it they need to get off the block and stop hiding out around kids. They know what they doing when they do that!"

I remember that conversation like yesterday, and little buddy was, as we say, "popped." Some of these young men are that far gone, and only God can save them at that point. It hurt to watch, but he was in a place where neither I nor anyone else could say or do anything that could help him, so I let him be without saying another word.

It was four months before my release date and I was still troubled by not finishing my associate's degree. For some reason I just couldn't let it go. Right on time, like magic, a reentry summit was being held in the gym, and information about going to college was available. I went to the counselor's office and asked him if there was anything I could take, just to add one more course on file. He pulled up my school records and showed me all the classes I had taken. My eyes bulged. I didn't realize I had taken so many. Not counting my constructional-occupation class that I received a certificate in, I had forty-three transferable credit hours. I was better off than I thought possible.

I took the information I had just received from the counselor over to the reentry summit and went to the table that was explaining the qualifications for student financial aid. The woman at the table told me that if I qualified, much of my schooling, if not all, could be paid for. Because I had no intention of doing anything but finish school when I got home, I took that student financial-aid form back to the cell house and called Carrie to tell her about the information I had just got. Excitedly, I told her about my plans to send the forms out, and she suggested that they be submitted online because not only would it be faster, it was how the world pretty much did business these days. I agreed, and ten minutes later everything was completed and sent to wherever it needed to go. After our conversation I went to my cell, filled out the form I had, and put it in the mail anyway. I had never seen the Internet before, had no idea how it worked, and was not about to chance my future on something I didn't understand.

At thirty days from release, I kept to myself so I could work through everything that was about to happen. Unless the people were in the immediate circle of men I considered good friends, I didn't speak much. I was taking it all in. Fifteen long years had come and gone, and now I was only days away from returning to my family. I sat in my cell and tried to read the books I'd been meaning to read, but the excitement was way too much. I increased my exercise to take away some of the eagerness, but there was nothing I could do, so I stayed up late at night, walking the halls and listening to my Walkman. My time had come to an end and I made it out with a revived spirit, a partial education, and my sanity. There were times throughout this prison sentence that I was unsure of myself. When things went wrong, I thought the burden was too great to bear. There is a verse in scripture that says, "Do people think that they will be left alone because they say: "We believe," and will not be tested?" Prison both tried and tested me, as it does every human being who comes through its gates, and although I have no idea what it did for other men, it made me a believer.

As a young man held captive in the penitentiary from age twenty to thirty-five, I had no choice but to adapt to survive. What must clearly register to anyone who reads this is what I was forced to adapt to. I had to adjust to psychotic madness. Abnormal behavior was considered normal behavior, and my mind had to absorb chaos and anarchy day after day after day after day for fifteen consecutive years. Although, and only through God's mercy, I fought off the horrific influences of prison culture, some of the mental conditioning I received from being exposed to that environment for so long a time was inevitable.

Epilogue

You know you

And I know you

We all know you

But you don't think we do

I knew you then

And they did too

So what makes you think that we don't know you

You do this, this, this, and this

I saw you then and I see you now

So trying to convince me of who you are is unnecessary!

—Yamini

The morning of June 20, 2011, I was released from Logan Correctional Center with three years of mandatory supervised release (parole). I said my goodbyes to men I considered brothers, whom I had been imprisoned with a long time. All of those years practicing good conduct and good character were about to be put to the real test.

I walked through the front gate carrying my belongings and saw a big SUV parked out front. The door swung open and my brother Bashir, two sisters Amia and Nisaa, and Ibrahim, my father, jumped out. My smile was so big it stretched the muscles in my jaw and hurt my face. I hadn't seen any of them in years, but I always spoke with them on the phone and in letters. After our hugs and a few pictures, I turned around and took one last look at the place where I had spent the last four years and an institution that had held me captive for fifteen years. The only thing I could think of was, "God, I hope I'm not a bug. I been in here too long with these maniacs and I may have a little maniac residue on me." I climbed into the truck and my brother pulled off. It was hard to believe that I was now a free man in the city.

We had a two-and-a-half-hour drive back to Chicago, so we stopped at a local McDonald's where I could change out of the prison sweats I was wearing and put on some real clothes. It had been a long time since I'd been in a public place, and my senses let me know immediately. Nervously, I walked into the building carrying the bag my brother brought me and went to the bathroom to change. The door was closed, and instead of me entering it as normal people do, I knocked. Bashir fell out laughing. "It's going be all right, man," he said. "We gon' get you straightened out. It's a public bathroom. You can walk right in."

After I got dressed, I came out into the restaurant area and felt like everybody was watching me. I was thinking, "This is the prison town. I'm big, black, and nervous. Everybody in here knows I just got out." Feeling extremely uncomfortable, I hurried up and got back in the truck.

The drive to my mother's house was full of conversation between us all and was the quickest two and a half hours of my life. When we pulled up to my mother's house, I sat there in the front seat and stared at the home I was raised in. It was a dream. Taking a deep breath, I stepped out of the truck and looked down the block in both directions. The scene was overwhelming. Summer was just beginning and people's lawns were manicured with plush green grass and decorated with beautiful, colorful flowers. Homes lined up in rows and rows and had children playing outside several of them. One man was washing his car and another was in his driveway doing some mechanical work on his. I held back tears thinking about the smallest things that spending almost a generation in prison had snatched from me. Somewhere a dog was barking, and it added to the scene I was observing of people living decently.

Slowly I walked to the front door and took another deep breath before I opened it. Inside was a house full of family: my brother, sisters, nieces, both parents, Carrie, the woman I fell in love with, and people I've known all my life who too were family. In this room were the people who cared for me, supported me, and encouraged me my entire fifteen years in prison. They never neglected or abandoned me and were part of the reason I made it through that long, dismal journey without an angry, frustrated mind. This was my support group, my reentry team, and after everything they'd done for me, they still understood that their jobs were not yet finished. They were all unselfishly preparing to help me help myself to become the man they all knew I had the potential of becoming.

My mother, the woman who raised me to be the man that I became, hugged me so strong I couldn't hold the tears any longer. She couldn't take seeing her oldest son in a cage, and for that reason I only saw her twice my entire prison sentence. Her letters never wavered, though, and week after week they came like clockwork, reminding me of who I was and encouraging me to continue to remain a decent, God-fearing human being in spite of my surroundings. "So what," she would say. "Believers influence their environments; they are not influenced by them." I lived on those words.

Our reunion at my mother's house was short because I had a small window to meet and greet everyone. I was on house arrest and had to get to Carrie's apartment, the place that I had registered to live with the parole board. The house arrest was for four months and was exactly what I needed to absorb all of this new information. Being in the world again, I was a fish out of water and had to regain my sensitivities to women and children and everything else. I came home to a world that did not exist when I left it, and sitting in front of Carrie's computer, I saw two things for the very first time in my life: the Internet and an email.

Clueless, amazed, and needing to learn how technology works, I played around with the computer while Carrie was at work. I went to a friend of mine's Web site to check out what he'd been doing, and something popped up on the screen telling me I may have won one million dollars. Curious, and having no knowledge of what not to do, I clicked on the pop-up and downloaded a virus to her computer, completely destroying it. It was the beginning of many costly accidents that came from having no knowledge of technology or how the world operates.

Now that I was home, I was given a cell phone to be able to communicate with everyone whenever I needed to. The problem was that I had no idea how to use the thing. I couldn't even turn it on to answer it when it rang. Imani, Carrie's five-year-old daughter, whom I have known since birth from her and her mother's many visits, had to teach me how to operate it.

A couple of weeks passed and I was still getting familiar with my new surroundings; however, Carrie was becoming very frustrated with me. I was manhandling everything in the small apartment and breaking her belongings. In prison everything is steel and concrete, so there's very little damage that can be done to state property. I was not used to handling delicate things, so she banned me from touching anything other than the TV remote and the refrigerator when she wasn't home. For some reason I didn't take the time to figure out how things worked. If something didn't fit, I would force it instead of turning it the proper way. I couldn't figure out why I was in such a hurry to do things. It wasn't my normal behavior, and I was growing frustrated with myself.

As my frustration increased, I began to forget the simplest things people said to me, or forget things I had recently done. I was leaving the water running in the bathroom, causing overflows in the sink and tub, or setting the milk cap on top of the container so that when Carrie picked it up, assuming it was closed, it spilled all over the place. One night I went to bed leaving the back door completely open—not unlocked, wide open. I thought something was wrong with me. I thought I was having a nervous breakdown of some sort for forgetting to do things that are natural reactions. I was being hit with so much brand-new information from this new world that I was having a systems overload, and I wanted to go see a counselor.

It was a rough few weeks, but Carrie and I weathered the storm together, and on August 17, 2011, fifty-eight days after my release, she and I were married. We bought a home not far from our apartment to start our new life together, and where my wonderful new wife gave me time, space, and support to adjust to this new environment.

My adjustment was another experience in itself. Because I had been around nothing but hardened men for fifteen years, I sometimes responded to my wife like I would a man in a prison cell. If ever she was saying something I didn't like or didn't agree with, I would look away and not give her eye contact, treating her as if she didn't exist. Whenever she asked me to do what I thought was one too many things, like take out the garbage, bring the groceries from the car, or cut the grass, I would have an attitude and feel as if she were demanding too much, like a prison guard. One day, I was leaving the house and she asked me a simple question that a wife asks her husband: "Babe, where are you going?" I snapped back, "I'm a free man. I'm going wherever the hell I want to."

I hated behaving like that, and I couldn't figure out why I was doing it. My wife called me an insensitive jerk, and it threatened our relationship. She needed a husband to show her love and affection, and Imani needed a father, not a drill sergeant. Sadly, I had no idea how.

In most prisons in the state of Illinois, unless a person is isolated in segregation, he is not alone. There was always a cellmate, or two or three. It was hard to find a peaceful space where I could be alone, undisturbed, with my thoughts. I spent most of the early months after my release in another room, away from other people, because I enjoyed the solitude so much. Even though I was in the house, the only time my wife and I spoke was when I wanted something.

I hated what prison had done to me emotionally. It snatched away those sensitivities that I needed for women and children and desensitized me to certain emotions necessary to have a good, healthy relationship.

I thank God for everything in my life, especially my wife. It takes a special, special woman to put up with the emotional detachment of a man who has spent so many years in prison. Without the faith she has in me, in my character, and in my willingness to work on regaining those lost sensitivities, our relationship wouldn't stand a chance. It's too much to ask. It's too draining.

When I was released from house arrest in December of 2011, I contacted the colleges that serviced the prisons where I had taken courses for my transcripts. For years I had lain on my bunk fantasizing about going to an accredited university and not a small college, although the smaller ones were smart financial decisions. Two weeks after I contacted the schools, my transcripts arrived, and with my wife's urging, I called UIC (University of Illinois at Chicago) admissions to find out if and how I could get into their College of Liberal Arts and Sciences. The information I was given by UIC's counselors said that I needed to meet a few academic requirements to qualify that I didn't have in my transcripts. Without hesitation or discouragement, I immediately found out what those requirements were, and three weeks later, on January 20, 2012, I enrolled at Triton College, a school on UIC's list of small colleges that it accepted credits from. I was now a college student.

Completely broke, jobless, a newlywed, and living off of my wife's income, I walked into the financial-aid office at Triton wondering how in the world this education was going to get paid for. My wife had been financially supporting everything I was involved in, and I was beginning to feel like a huge burden. As I filled out the "broke as hell" forms, a counselor stood over me, watching as I marked off sections that exposed how much I wasn't contributing to my household. The questions about my empty pockets were killing me. Me and my pride were having a fight, and I was getting dealt with. Drowning in shame, I handed the form to the counselor as she picked up a brochure about student-worker programs. In it were janitorial jobs and other small details around the campus for people to help pay for their tuition. Turning toward me, she opened her mouth to say something, but before she got out a word I said in a tone that may have been a bit sharp, "The only toilet I will ever clean again is the one in my house, but thank you."

Understanding where I was coming from, she smiled and said, "Oookay, I'm just saying. Any little bit helps."

We walked over to the computer so the counselor could upload my financial-aid form, and when she opened my file she found that I had already been approved for a grant for the maximum amount for the current school year. The file said that the aid had been approved eight months ago. Sitting there speechless from joy but confused about how this could possibly be, my memory returned to the penitentiary when I submitted my financial-aid application from the cellhouse. Yep!

Going in I knew school was going to be challenging, but I survived prison. The courses I needed were philosophy, humanities, a science with a lab, economics, and another social science. Sitting in a real classroom for the first time since high school was an experience I didn't expect. I was surrounded by young students, kids seventeen and eighteen years old, who were all infants when I was arrested in 1996. I was the old man in the room—older than one of my professors.

My classes were going well and I maintained a 3.6 GPA; however, the requirements that I was fulfilling for UIC weren't enough. At the last minute, I found out that I still had to be accepted by admissions at the university, so I wrote a sincere letter to UIC explaining my prison circumstance, the efforts I made with young men while I was there, and the work with young people I planned to continue. The response I received from the university was so quick it caught me by surprise. Before I was halfway through the semester at Triton College, the University of Illinois at Chicago accepted me into its College of Liberal Arts and Sciences to pursue a degree in sociology. God is greater!

In the summer of 2012, one year after my release from prison, I took my passion for helping young men recognize the value in being a dignified human being and, with the support of my family, I founded Determined To Be UpRight, a nonprofit 501(c)(3) organization whose goal is to enable our young men to become upright in both their thinking and behavior. Remembering myself at ages twelve through eighteen made me want to target young men those ages who want to be free to grow into family and community assets and not become candidates for gang recruitment.

At the same time that DTBU was being established, again with the support of my family, I also founded my publishing company, "The Proper Perception", that also conducts speaking engagements on the reality of the prison experience without any romanticism or glorification. It is a powerful presentation that our young people must see.

Any person who may have the urge to go against the established laws of society and receives a long prison sentence will be exposed to the harsh, vulgar, volatile, emotionless, and sanity-threatening culture of prison life. This is true regardless of gender, class, race, level of education, professional position, or religious affiliation.

Many men are paroled to halfway houses when they are released, but most of them return to family members without the family's proper understanding of "who" and in some cases "what" they just invited into their homes. The after-effects of these long prison sentences are just as damaging as the horrible experience itself. The former prisoner is not the same person the family once knew. Their conversations, thinking, and behavior may be so intolerable that it will have you asking on a daily basis, "What's Wrong With You?"